CRICKET, ADVANCE!

Remember, in studying the pictures in this book, that I am a left-hander. Although hooking the ball really hard, complete balance is kept. Head and eyes right, wrists have rolled over, pivoting on back foot. Test v. England, Nottingham 1957.

CRICKET, ADVANCE!

Gary Sobers

PELHAM BOOKS

First published by
PELHAM BOOKS LTD
26 Bloomsbury Street
*London, W.C.*1
1965

2532

Made and printed in Great Britain by
Thomas Nelson (Printers) Ltd London and Edinburgh

CONTENTS

Foreword by Sir Donald Bradman   7

Preface by Sir Frank Worrell   9

1   GENERAL COACHING   11

2   BATTING   15

3   BOWLING   35

4   FIELDING   51

5   WICKETKEEPING   67

6   CAPTAINCY   75

7   SOBER REFLECTIONS: *Past, Present and Future*   91

FOREWORD

by Sir Donald Bradman

SOME years ago, Sir Leary Constantine was in Australia and I sought his views on the young and up-and-coming Gary Sobers. When he told me Sobers was the hardest hitter of a ball he had ever seen I really sat up and took notice for the great Constantine himself was such a tremendous striker of the ball.

Today, after having seen Gary Sobers over a few seasons, I think Sir Leary was right in his assessment.

With his long grip of the bat, his high back lift and free swing, I think, by and large, Gary Sobers consistently hits the ball harder than anyone I can remember.

This helps to make him such an exciting batsman to watch, because the emphasis is on power and aggression rather than technique—the latter being the servant, not the master. The uncoiling of those strong, steely wrists, as he flicks the ball wide of mid-on, is a real joy to watch because it is unique and superbly controlled, whilst the full-blooded square cut is tremendous.

Sobers' record entitles him to be ranked with the world's great batsmen. And I should think he could find a place in any Test team as a bowler, firstly as a more than lively swinger and seamer, reverting to spinners (with one of the most deceptive of all googlies) when the occasion warrants.

His glorious, full-shouldered, swinging bowling action is a model of fluency and such a welcome contrast to the many jerky and dubious actions we have witnessed in recent years.

Add to this the most astounding slip fielding, where his reactions are so swift that few people realise how difficult are those catches he nonchalantly throws up. At slip he most certainly ranks with the greatest we have ever seen.

Summing up, Sobers is a gloriously vital and exciting cricketer who gives full reign to his natural ability, to the delight of the public and in the true spirit of cricket.

Since he first came to South Australia I have been closely associated with Gary and my admiration for his ability and his approach to the game has grown each year. How often have I run my fingers through his curly hair in the dressing-room and asked for a hundred, and how often has he obliged. His consistency has in fact been quite astonishing considering the risks he is always prepared to take.

Has there ever been a greater all-rounder? That is a hard question to answer because it naturally calls to mind Davidson, Miller, Lindwall, Hammond, Rhodes and a host of others.

Cricket, thank goodness, is full of such imponderables, but if I were a Queen's Counsel, pleading his cause, I think I would find Sobers' case as easy to fight as that of anyone else.

Irrespective of these arguments I know that Sobers has given me the most enormous pleasure, and whenever he plays I

The stance. This is how I stand. Relaxed, attentive, comfortable, and in position to play back or forward with equal ease

shall always be there to watch him if I can.

Remember the old story of the coach who said to his pupil ' look where your feet are ', to be greeted with the response ' look where the ball is '. Sobers' feet are not always where the purist would decree, but what of it when the ball is rattling the pickets.

In the final analysis matches are won by runs, not theories, and I make no apology for admitting I am a Sobers' fan.

We need players of his type. They make cricket live.

Watching the ball, eyes following its direction just after I have steered Alan Davidson to third man in the Third Test at Sydney 1961

PREFACE

by SIR FRANK WORRELL

I WAS delighted when Gary Sobers was appointed captain of West Indies as my successor. This was the choice I most wanted, not only because Gary is such a fine cricketer.

His skills are known well enough not to require elaboration here. What he also possesses is a sheer, uninhibited love of the game, and a keen analytical cricket mind.

It was because of these attributes, as for his brilliant ability, that I was always grateful to have Gary alongside me on the field. I shall continue to derive immense satisfaction watching him from the boundary.

The next best thing to watching Sobers is reading about him. Here we get something good from both worlds, for through the illustrations in this book, and Sobers' own decided views, we are taken out there into the middle with him.

I commend this book to everyone who appreciates the good and right things there are in cricket; for no-one possesses them in greater measure than Garfield Sobers.

CHAPTER ONE

GENERAL COACHING

THIS might appear a curious opening statement to make in a book dealing with the technique of cricket, but I have to be frank and say I do not believe in too much coaching! Good coaching, yes; but anything less tends to coach people out of things rather than into a fuller evolution of all their natural abilities. The first essential towards becoming a cricketer is to love the game, as I shall emphasise all the way through.

At the very beginnings, I think there is a real danger that coaching can be made too much like school lessons. A boy should not think he is being taught to play cricket; he should feel he is taking part in a game. This starts from the simple joy of chucking a ball about, catching it, hitting it and fetching it, and is one reason why I am not too sure about so much of this group coaching. Done properly, and in strictly limited doses, of course, it is very useful, but I often think I prefer to see the kids enjoying themselves with a lemonade bottle and a tennis ball in the intervals of first-class matches. Loving the game is the key to it all.

Enthusiasm for the game has first to be nurtured, then when you are sure that your pupil really wants to play with a ball, the rudiments of the game can be introduced. Batting and bowling in a net can be tedious and dull. So can group fielding practice, although it helps to develop the patience that is a vital part of any cricketer's make-up.

Consequently, I am heavily in favour of a few diversions to a coaching routine. Enjoyable exercises such as football, handball, skipping and baseball, can help co-ordination in cricket. Skipping, in particular, gets the legs moving more quickly, and helps to get the feet going more lightly, bearing in mind that a cricketer's feet are among the most important tools of his trade. For this reason, dancing is also a useful diversion, recalling a famous comment which has been round the world thousands of times: ' You gotta have rhythm! '

A steady head and quick feet are the

Climbing into a full-toss at Lord's in 1957. The feet, eyes and
follow-through have helped me hit it wide and over mid-on

Fred Trueman's late inswinger does me no good at Edgbaston, 1963.
I don't suppose a right-handed batsman would have appreciated it, either

basic physical requirements for cricket. Surprisingly, it has to be stressed time and again, that the head almost invariably should be kept in the same position when going through a stroke, and also when bowling and fielding. You often hear that a batsman is bowled through ' lifting his head '. This is perfectly true. But you can also miss a catch . . . fail to achieve a run-out . . . bowl a loose delivery . . . through throwing the head out of alignment.

I have talked about the feet and the head as being the vital things to get right in cricket. This, of course, means that position and balance will be right too.

Getting all these correct give you a firm basis of sound technique, and from then on it is up to you to build upon that technique to make yourself a good, effective cricketer.

Cricketers from my home, Barbados, have a wonderful opportunity to develop their cricket—possibly better than any other place. Not many people there are born with silver spoons in their mouths, although the sugar they produce keeps plenty of spoons busy all the time.

What we have are nature's wonderful privileges. A marvellous climate; brilliantly good and clear light; and this love of cricket that grows because the opportunity is there to play and enjoy it.

Most important of all, perhaps, we have the pitches on which we can seek to practise and make perfect. We have them because we work hard to prepare them. The climate helps, but you can never get a good wicket unless it is concrete or matting, without a lot of elbow grease and sweat.

These wickets are obviously good for the batsmen because the ball comes through fast and true, and encourages a player to pick up his bat and really let it go through. It is good for bowlers because they learn the first essentials of control, of length and direction, and also the right philosophy to the game. It is better for the fielders because firm strokes are being played, and there is an exciting challenge not only to cut down the runs but also to pick up the more frequent chances that follow stroke play.

We get the best pitches in the world simply because the groundsman at home always has plenty of men to help him with his preparation, and because they are up at six o'clock in the morning, to start and carry on rolling, rolling, rolling.

In contrast, in England I often find that pitches are under-prepared and the reason is simply a lack of labour. This too often means that batsmen cannot trust the pitch; fielders consequently haven't much to do; and medium-paced bowlers bang away just short of a length, waiting for the pitch to get them their wickets.

It is easy to write it, I know, but making your practice and match wickets as good as you possibly can will bring back a great deal of the enjoyment and challenge to a

Talking to my brother Gerry, who plays League cricket for the Staffordshire club, Norton

game which sometimes seems short of these important commodities.

This is a vital part of making coaching positive and not negative. Before you can get very far, you must have mastered the fundamentals of feet, head, position and balance, and brought them into your cricket—in every phase.

Having established a fairly sound launching platform for a cricket future, you will want to 'get off the ground' by developing your own tastes and choices, things that fit your own mind and body better than anything else. This is positive coaching. It offers to teach you how to do things properly rather than saying bleakly: "You mustn't do that."

Once having made your coaching positive, play your cricket the same way. Be ready always to attack, to take a firm grip of the game by your own positive methods whenever a decent opportunity arises. Only experience will tell you when this is, but watch and learn from all the good players you can. Adventurous cricket, which has, of necessity, to be based on solid foundations, is the most glorious of all cricket to play in. If it is not firmly based, it just becomes a boring pantomime to anyone who really appreciates and understands it.

I don't know what they mean by 'brighter cricket'. What we want is *better* cricket, which invariably means a game full of challenge, counter-challenge, tactics and counter-tactics—a joy to play in and a delight to watch.

In due course, we shall be looking into fundamental cricket techniques, cricket tactics and strategy, and all sorts of what I would call 'the mechanics' of the game.

I would like to end this little preamble by mentioning the spirit of cricket. All over the world, whenever a person sees something that is a bit shady, very sharp, downright dishonest, or in general a 'bit off', they say just one phrase. No other game has ascended to such a height as is shown in the universally used and completely understood three words 'it's not cricket'.

After a year or two playing the game, you will not need a text-book definition of it, any more than you will need an explanation of what exactly it means on the cricket field.

A true cricketer has an instinctive feeling for what is, and is not, cricket. A true cricketer will protect and abide by these all-powerful, unwritten laws to the end of his days, regardless of the cost to him or his side.

Let us, then, get on to playing cricket.

A discussion on coaching with Ron Roberts, the famous cricket writer (left) and William Luscombe, Editorial Director of Pelham Books (right)

CHAPTER TWO

BATTING

THE object of batting is to make enough runs to enable your bowlers to win the game for you. I feel this obvious truth is often forgotten in a mass of theory and elaborate witch-craft which baffles the ordinary cricketer.

Of course, we all like to see correct, graceful strokes, but it is no good to the side if there are not enough of them. Plenty of very useful players have been a bit clumsy, with flaws in their technique, but they have overcome them by graft and concentration, and made themselves much more valuable to the side.

Trevor Bailey, of course, had a fine Test record for England. There were no flaws in his technique, certainly not defensively, but he made himself a far more useful player at top level by accepting his limitations and playing within them and also by showing what a good temperament he had in his love of a scrap. One of Bailey's weaknesses—as a scorer at any rate—was that he could not force strongly off the back foot. He was essentially a front-foot player, and of Bailey more than

any other the maxim ' when in doubt push out ' held good.

Ken Barrington is a more recent example of a batsman who has accepted, even imposed, limitations on himself. I think sometimes English batsmen are too inclined to do this but, of course, they do have to play under more variable conditions than the majority of overseas players. Ken originally won his spurs as an out-and-out stroke maker, but he could not hold a Test place. When he did so he developed more in the ' sheet anchor ' role. The figures he has achieved for England since then speak for themselves.

In the West Indies we are not keen to have so many ' blockers ', but even we accept that you have to have a balance between those belting the cover off the ball, and those whose job it is to wear out the bowlers for the knock-out punch. Joe Solomon is one of this type, and although he is a fine stroke maker in his own right, Conrad Hunte played the more solid type of role to important effect in the 1963 series in England.

England have now got another young batsman who looks like becoming a top ranker because of his dedication and concentration. He is Geoff Boycott, with whom I had the pleasure of sharing in a double-century partnership when I was a guest player with Yorkshire in a delightful week in Bermuda towards the end of 1964. This partnership was made on a matting pitch spread over concrete so that the ball bounced higher and faster than usual. Boycott impressed me by his thoughtfulness in adapting himself. First he changed his usual short-handled bat for a long-handled one (and it pleased me, of course, that he happened to borrow one of mine!), and he also altered his grip so that his bottom hand was higher on the bat's handle. This meant there was less chance of him being hit on the knuckles. Boycott has the reputation for being an ordinary player in the nets, but he certainly knows how to make runs when it comes to the crunch.

Incidentally, Geoff and some of the other Yorkshire boys were surprised that I watched so little when not actually batting. I picked up the habit from Frank Worrell, who explained, " If you watch another batsman out there in the middle struggling, he is apt to give you the impression the bowling is better than it is." I agree with Frank that batting being an individual exercise in many ways, it is best not to have pre-conceived theories and instead to go out there and play each ball on its merits. However, for young players making their way and seeking to improve, watching established players obviously has important educational value. Let's revert, though, to the nets.

I know of dozens of batsmen who look world-beaters in the nets, when there is no pressure (and no fielders!), but fail continually in the middle.

Some measure of success is vital to keeping interest in the game, and that is why you must have a reasonably sound defence to do anything at all for any length of time. If you can stay in for a while in your early cricketing days, you will get the confidence to begin going for your shots and, gradually, taking over the initiative from the bowlers. These things need plenty of practice, and nobody will go far without it.

The vital things about batting are position and balance, always assuming that you have a fairly good ' eye for a ball '. Most people have some ball sense, and you will find that people good at one ball game can usually do pretty well at another. I played nearly every sort of game when I was young, and especially enjoyed table tennis. Ken Mackay, the Australian, and the English opener, Geoff Pullar, gave me plenty of good games, and I think they helped to sharpen up my reflexes.

I am a great believer in ' shadowing '. This means taking up your batting positions, and practising them without a ball, rather as they do in shadow boxing. It is perfectly feasible to improve your cricket without a ball. If you get the ' feel ' of doing things the right way, you won't have to think about them in the middle. They will come automatically. Playing with a tennis ball is also useful exercise. As it bounces higher, it gives you more of a test on the short-pitched ball, teaching you how to hook and pull, and keep the ball on the ground.

I sometimes think that English coaches concentrate too much on teaching young players to deal with well-pitched-up balls first, but I suppose if many of them have been brought up on rough, fiery pitches, you have to start somewhere building up their confidence to hit the ball on a good wicket.

Definitely not advised. I have had a real slash at Len Coldwell, but it was a no-ball, so it only cost my side three runs. South Australia v M.C.C., Adelaide, 1962

The stance. Head and eyes watching bowler over shoulder. Well-balanced, with weight even on both feet, which are both level with crease

Position of hands on bat. Top wrist faces mid-off to give me full scope for the drives. This is the guide. The bottom hand gives the punch, brought in at the right time

This is playing back to a ball just short of a length. Back foot has gone back to cover the middle stump. Bat has been taken straight back, ensuring a straight path downwards to meet the ball. Shoulder is in line with the pitch of the ball

As the ball hits the bat, the handle is sloped towards the bowler, making sure it stays on the carpet. The ball drops straight down, away from any close 'sharks' who are looking for the careless shot

Defensive forward shot, to a ball fairly well up but not far enough up to punish. Top hand has turned on the bat, the bottom hand is completely relaxed (to prevent any edge carrying to close fielders). Head and eyes are well down, shoulder is well over the ball. Weight on front foot, knee bent

Position of the hands at the time of impact in forward defence. Top hand has turned on the handle, is forcing the handle forward and down. Bottom hand is just making sure that the whole thing is right to drop the ball down out of harm's way

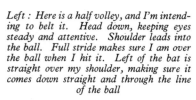

Left : Here is a half volley, and I'm intending to belt it. Head down, keeping eyes steady and attentive. Shoulder leads into the ball. Full stride makes sure I am over the ball when I hit it. Left of the bat is straight over my shoulder, making sure it comes down straight and through the line of the ball

Right : Just after the drive : ' leaning into ' the ball, guiding with my top hand. At moment of striking bottom hand comes in hard to give the real power. Head and eyes are still on the line of the ball. No ' pulling away ' to get extra power into the shot. Bat goes right through, the full arc, giving maximum power to the stroke

Left : The straight drive follows much the same principles as the cover drive, and here is the end of one, demonstrating again the importance of a good, full, follow-through

Right : Good follow-through but not a good shot. I am too upright, with eyes not examining the ball closely enough. Ball was not really ' there ' to be driven, and I had to make it up as I went along!

Left : Same stroke as above. My weight is not really into the stroke. I should probably have done better off the back foot, giving myself a chance to look at the ball off the pitch

Right : The on-drive. A very difficult shot to play properly. My method is to push the foot out, as with the other drives, and to have my head over the top of the ball when I hit it

19

However, even after my international career began, I found I could achieve something by tennis-ball practice, and I frequently did. One great advantage for youngsters, of course, is that it does not hurt!

I have said that batting means run-getting, so let's look at it very closely and simply. Supposing you are playing in a club or school match as a batsman. Usually your first target should be to make fifty runs, a very useful score.

To make that many, you will probably have to face a hundred balls of all sorts, any one of which can get you out in nine legitimate ways. Some reckon there are ten ways, including 'jockeyed out'!

In that hundred balls, the odds are that only fifty can be reasonably safe to score from. The others you will have to 'block', although even then, with good anticipation and a good partner, you will be able to get a few sharp singles. This is always a way to flummox a bowler, and to begin to break his field up into ways he does not fancy at all.

It is all up to you. You are on your own in the middle, and one mistake can mean the end of your innings. It only ever took one ball to get rid of the greatest batsman in the world.

You must select your scoring strokes, try your present form, and try eventually to dictate your own terms to the bowlers. You do not make an innings with a few flashy shots. You build it up consciously and carefully, getting yourself attuned to the light, the state of the pitch, the bowlers and the condition of the game as you go along.

In general, I do not care for inflexible rules, but there is one you must stick to, as long as you are in. Watch the ball, watch the ball, watch the ball. This does not simply mean a look at it when it starts off its flight. You watch it on to the bat, study it, stare at it, become fascinated by it. As the old players used to say, 'smell it', meaning that it is right there under your nose, under your command.

Another rule to be observed is 'get on to the line' as soon as you can. This is position, which is dictated by your feet, almost your most important assets. Your brain tells your feet to go, they move your body into the right line, the head and eyes are on the right spot to deal with things, and you've got a great start towards making your strokes.

Getting your body on the line and picking the bat up at twelve o'clock means your bat will swing straight through the line of the ball, and not across it. Hitting across the line of the ball makes timing a great deal harder, and missing a lot easier.

At the beginning of your knock, you will be anxious to get the 'feel' of everything. Study the wicket, and the bowler's angle of delivery, and watch how he is trying to get you out. I always look at the bowler's hand all the time just as he is coming up to his delivery stride. If I find my concentration is wandering at all, I go down the pitch and pat it down, just to give myself a chance to 'tighten up' again. I know one player, who, whenever he finds himself puzzled by a bowler, takes hold of himself by thinking, 'He won't get me out this ball'.

Although all bad balls cannot be safely dispatched, you can make your mark by belting the first bad one you do get. A swinging full toss, for instance, is a useful delivery to bowl to a new batsman, trying to get off the mark, but if he does hammer it, he has won an important point over the bowler.

All this comes back to the confidence you get from your practice, with or without the ball. Many of your movements

20

Frank Worrell, captain of the West Indies in the great Test series in Australia and England

will be automatic, and you can just concentrate on that vital thing—watching the ball.

I will always argue with many coaches who say such things as 'you shouldn't cut, hook or pull'. I think that young players should be taught how to play them safely and profitably, not just wash them out because there is danger there. Coaching, to my mind, must be positive, not negative.

If you find your driving working well, then you should get into a net and build up against your weaknesses. If you like to cut and hook, go into a net, and ask your bowlers to test you. It is no good bowling two dozen half-volleys to a chap who can drive like a horse but cannot play back to save his life. If he has any sense, he will have gone into a net to try to sort out his weak spots, not just to demonstrate to himself something he knew very well before.

Although it is clearly safer to score your runs along the ground, there's a lot to be said for hitting the ball in the air. Here again, sensible practice gives the confidence and feel of doing it properly, and hitting in the air, after all, is just an extension of hitting along the ground.

A stroke in the air played with the head down, the feet in the right place and a full follow-through can be as safe as the ground shot, if played properly. It is as well to remember that it gives a bowler very serious food for thought if he finds himself being safely, properly and firmly hit back over his head. If it happens after an 'eyes-closed' slog, however, he will be lifted in morale, rightly reckoning he's got the batsman in a pretty desperate state.

Either shot establishes who is boss of the situation.

Besides practice, with someone of experience watching, I have found the best way to learn is by listening. I still listen to the talk in Test match dressing-rooms and find I can usually learn from it, after I have sorted out and rejected the various fallacies that come out.

I think I learned most about batting in the early stages of my career from Arthur Morris, the great Australian opener, who was also a left-hander.

He and Neil Harvey were the great left-handers of the period, and after I had been picked for Barbados against the 1955 Australians I looked at Arthur more closely than I have ever studied a batsman before. He made the game look so easy, always the hallmark of greatness. I have read a lot about him shuffling across the line of the ball, but reckon a lot of hot air is talked about that.

To me, he was basically correct, because here was a batsman who anticipated length and direction almost by instinct, and was always in the right position. I had every reason to respect his quality in the years and challenges to come.

At first sight I was not so impressed with Harvey. I think it was because he played his cover drive with his foot a long way from the ball. What I perhaps did not understand just then was that he was such an intelligent player that he realised he could get away with it on our perfect pitches. In fact, most of the English bowlers of my time have said that Neil was the best player they knew among the Australians on a turning pitch. In these circumstances he was so quick to get down the pitch to smother the spin, and also knew all about getting right back on to his stumps to handle the shorter one. He was completely positive about this, right forward or right back, no half measures, and it showed his great adaptability to different pitches.

Still, as I say, the player who made the big impression on me was Morris, because of his effortless positioning, footwork and speed to get behind the line of flight.

Naturally, one of my idols was Frank Worrell, and another, Everton Weekes, both of whom I had watched since the age of six. I do not suppose I could have chosen a better model than Frank, who was to captain us in those great series in Australia and England, and perhaps in my formative days I was inclined to be a bit blinded by hero worship. Nevertheless, by trying to imitate him, I certainly got a wonderful grounding in batting, and when Frank left Barbados, Everton took over as my hero-in-chief.

Everton was a complete cricketer, for the joy of the game exuded from him in the brilliant smile he never seemed to lose. It must have looked a savage grin, however, to opposing bowlers, many of whom said he was the one 'W' they least liked to bowl against.

For artistry and fluency there is no doubt that Worrell was the master—he possessed such a beautiful technique. But for power and strength I do not suppose any batsman has hit the ball harder than Clyde Walcott. Brian Statham recalls fielding one of Clyde's specials, played off the back foot—after it had hit the concrete wall behind the bowler and rebounded to him! Weekes, however, was so nimble in his movements and reflexes that he could get into a position to play all the shots with an unrelenting savagery that no other player could quite match. Perhaps he was also prepared to give the bowlers a chance, but when he was in form, which was practically every innings between 1947 and 1952, he was a shining star all on his own.

Everton was my first captain in an overseas trip, for we had a tour of Bermuda from Barbados in the early fifties when I was still very, very green. The advice Everton gave me then put my first foot firmly on the lowermost rungs of the ladder all cricketers must attempt to climb. Such was Everton's enthusiasm for the game that several years after he had played his last match for the West Indies he went on a 40,000-mile tour with a Commonwealth team in 1962. He covered all this ground in eight weeks and I believe played one or two innings right out of the top drawer. All the players jestingly called him ' father ' because he was the senior member when Ray Lindwall was injured. He also skippered the side with, as I understand it, great distinction, for one of Everton's secrets is that he has been able to laugh with, as well as at, the world.

He became friendly on that trip with Roy McLean the South African batsman, which underlines that sportsmen can, given the chance, break through political barriers. Together they enjoyed a joke with an Australian taxi-driver who asked them if they were members of a South African team. " Man are you colour blind ? " replied Everton.

Back to those early days—I left school at fourteen and went into Barbados League cricket. I was still a little fellow and not allowed to play in City cricket. I played for a country team and did well. I fancy this makes an important point—not to get out of your own class in cricket, or in anything else, too quickly. This is one of the advantages of the Australian system, which is graded so thoroughly from school cricket right up to International level.

I eventually played for a country team against one from the City, got a few wickets (I did not bat much in those days) and was picked to play for the Combined Barbados Country and City League XI

A short one at the body and I have decided to hook. The movement of the back foot has just started towards the off-stump and the bat will soon get to the 12 o'clock position

I have moved just inside the line of the ball, and my whole weight is just about to get on to my back foot. It is just pivoting to get the full weight behind it. It is important to get the weight on that back foot as soon as possible, giving a firm base for the shot

The complete follow-through for the hook. This is a fine and satisfying stroke which needs perfect balance and judgment for safe and effective results

My wrists have 'rolled over', so that, at the moment of impact the bat is facing downwards, keeping the ball down

against the Barbados Cricket Association. Our captain was in the police force, and I was invited to join the Police City team, which meant I had to join the police in some capacity. I joined as a band cadet, so I blew a bugle to play for my club.

Perhaps still thinking about my tennis-ball experiences, I got hit on the jaw trying to hook a short one from E. A. V. Williams in my first game of B.L.A. cricket in 1952. This naturally stopped me playing the bugle and I could not practise the following week. This upset my bandmaster with the result that my career in the Police team was very short-lived.

I do not suppose being unable to blow a bugle will get me dropped from another team, however long I play!

I am, however, not including any advice here about bugling for promising young players. Or blowing your own trumpet, for that matter.

Still, these early contacts with better players did me a world of good, and being a shy lad, it was about now that I realised how much I could learn by just watching and listening. Never be too proud to learn.

Before we move on to actual batting technique, a few words about equipment would not be out of place. As a general rule, you get what you pay for in cricket equipment as in anything else, and buying cheap stuff is usually false economy. As a matter of fact, a friend told me about a recent experience which makes the point neatly. The son of that noted Sussex batsman, H. W. Parks, and cousin of England's 'keeper Jim, was playing in a match in Devon. My friend noticed what a well-preserved and effective pair of pads he was wearing. " Yes," said the youngster, " Father has just passed them on to me. He told me he bought them just about thirty years ago."

Of course, when a young player is growing up rapidly, expensive gear can be a problem, as he will need new stuff every couple of seasons. When he is fully grown, however, my advice is to buy the best available. It not only adds to comfort, but it means that it will be looked after well, which all adds to its value.

Buying a bat is a very personal business. The tendency among the very young is to get bats which are far too big and heavy for young wrists and arms. Make sure that your bat fits your strength and your build. Have it light enough to be able to play your strokes without any great effort, and get an experienced cricketer to help you pick it out. Old cricketers always love doing this, remembering, no doubt, the thrill they used to get when young.

Select a nice straight-grained piece of wood which suits you for handle and balance. Only you can decide on the ' feel ' of a bat. You can pick up two dozen, and only one may feel exactly right. That's the one for you. When you have bought it, don't drown it in oil. A couple of light applications everywhere except the splice (one application on the back to keep the rain out!) will start you off. After each knock, lightly rub it down with fine sandpaper (to take away the marks of the edged shots and the old oil) and give another light oiling to the front, edges and toe.

If you can possibly avoid it, do not lend your bat.

This applies of course when you have only one bat. Professionals are a little more fortunate because they are able to make a selection through the help of manufacturers and so on. Indeed, a top-class player travelling the world needs to keep three or four bats in his possession. I have mentioned that for the player with a single bat his prize possession, he should lightly oil it and also keep it to himself. I should add here that I do not oil a bat at all in England, I just allow it to break itself in. In other words, I prefer to use a dry bat in a damp country, and merely use a fine-grain sandpaper to keep it clean. When in the West Indies or any other hot country, however, I do give my bats a bath in linseed oil because of the heat and evaporation. They would become too

and again, get the best you can, those which suit you best.

Always wear a ' box ', whether in matches or practice. This protects your private parts, and although it might seem uncomfortable in the first place, get used to it. There are several different types these days, and your ' old cricketer ' will be happy to advise you about them.

The rest of your cricket clothing is up to you and your resources. Boots, of

The leg glide. Played to a ball on the leg stump, with the bat perpendicular when it meets the ball. One should not try to 'flick' it towards fine leg. Meet it with the full blade, with the eyes completely in line, and it will give you a confident single without any risk, providing you have picked the right ball for the job

dry and tend to split without this treatment.

Pads should be picked for lightness, comfort and effectiveness. Do them up with buckles inside, the bottom one tight, the middle one fairly loose, and the top very loose. Do not have straps hanging loose. They can lead umpires to give you out caught behind, and look sloppy anyway. If you are lucky enough to have your own, cut off the straps so that the ends don't flop about.

Always wear batting gloves if you can,

course, are vital. Your feet get you into the right position for all your cricketing activities, and so must be absolutely right and comfortable.

I think it was Sir Pelham Warner who suggested that a pair of Sir Donald Bradman's boots should be put into a glass case at Lord's for posterity to gaze upon. Someone once likened Sir Donald's footwork to a ballet dancer's, so quickly did it always get him into the right position for everything he did on the field. Well, a lot of people thought the same.

Anyone with a chance to go to Lord's should look at a case outside the Secretary's office and next to the Committee Room. They will then see the Don's boots and better appreciate why he was so nimble and neat of foot.

Now that we are set up for the match, and assume we have won the toss, let's quietly get ready to go in.

Give yourself plenty of time to pad up, and if you like to, sit in the sun to get used to the light. My own idea is relaxation, like Worrell, in the pavilion.

When your turn comes, walk steadily in and take guard. This is a matter of personal taste, again, dictated by experience. Most take middle and leg or leg stump. If, as many batsmen are, you are a bit hazy on your leg stump, it is a useful tip to stand a little outside it, with your bat resting comfortably on the line of the leg stump. You then know anything bowled at your legs is off the stumps.

You look around at the field, noting where the close fielders are, and seeing where your run-savers are posted. This will give you an idea of what the bowler is trying to do to get you out.

You check that the sight-screen is right, and quietly settle down to receive the first ball. You watch the bowler run up, concentrate hard on his arm, and hand, and watch the ball as it comes towards you. It starts on off-stump, moving slightly away, and you move on to the line, covering up your stumps with your pads, lifting the bat out of any harm's way, and watch it go by.

He did not tempt you with that one.

The next one pitches on the middle stump, just short of a length. You go across to it, moving your back foot into line, with the bat back over your shoulder towards the twelve o'clock position. Leading on to the ball with your top hand and shoulder well over the top, you relax your grip with the bottom hand. You see it hit the bat; the ball trickles straight down and slowly out to cover. It is well wide of the bowler's follow-through and gully, and, as you have noted cover is a little deep, you call for a run as soon as you make the shot. Your partner responds immediately, completes the run easily, and you are ' off the mark '. Well done, I think you'll make a few today . . .

As your innings develops, you will get some long hops, half-volleys and the like, which offer good scoring chances, but the fact that you are still in depends on your ability to play the defensive strokes, forward and back. Head and eyes steady, feet to the ball and on the line of it, top hand and shoulder leading, bottom hand relaxed and helping the top to keep the ball down.

The orthodox attacking shots are mostly developments of these two fundamentals.

The drives are perhaps the most satisfactory of them. If you aim to get your front foot, fully extended, the ball, and the bat in the smallest possible area at the moment you hit the ball, you won't go far wrong. On the front-foot drives, the nearer you get your foot to the ball, and weight well forward, the less chance there is either of snicking the outswinger for a slip catch, or being clean bowled between bat and pad by the inswinger.

Forcing off the back foot brings in the same fundamentals, but, this time, you get most of your power from the bottom hand. You have moved fully back, in line with the ball, ' giving yourself room ', as they say, to get your wrists, arms, shoulders and back working in at the moment of the real punch. Still your head and eyes are steady, in line, with weight on back foot, ready to leave the ball, or change your shot, if the ball does

28

Norman O'Neill brings out a beautiful sweep against the chinaman that whistles for four

something unpleasant in the air or off the pitch.

Your back foot is almost parallel to the crease, and you may have to get up on tiptoe to get into the right spot to crack the ball down and hard. Experience—and that alone—will show you how to find the gaps in the field as you go into your shot with as much force as you can muster.

The most difficult of the drives is the on-drive, mainly because your front foot tends to get in the way of the straight flow of the bat. I say that there is no right or wrong way to do it, providing you are playing straight and the bat comes through straight and true. The right way for you is the way that brings you runs and does not get you out. Some players do not stretch too far. Their front foot goes forward a short distance, but head and eyes are still over the top of the ball when it is hit. My method is a development of this, as the picture shows, but I still reach forward as far as I can while still keeping balance and head steady.

One of the great tests of a good shot is whether or not the bat, if let go, would go the same place as the ball, and if the eyes are in the same direction. The great temptation is to alter your down swing and swish across the line of a straight one. This, obviously, can be disastrous.

There are, of course, plenty of strokes in which you have to hit across the line of the ball, but unless you are in tremendous form, or have made about eighty, they are not advisable against straight balls of good length.

The cut is played to a wide one outside the off stump. Your back foot carries your head and eyes to the line, and the bat comes down and across on top of the ball. You keep it down, and help it on its way.

Depending how fast and how far away from the wicket it is, you will cut fine or square of the wicket.

The hook is played to a short ball bouncing high over the wicket, somewhere near your body. You get into line with it, moving to your back foot, which is the pivot. Carrying on the movement, you get a little to the offside of the ball as it comes towards your head, and hit it as it passes.

A hook is a doubly risky shot in that it can lead to a batsman's dismissal and also to personal injury, but it is very satisfying to play effectively. It needs a brave batsman with quick reactions to hook properly. He must ensure that he gets inside the line of the ball and that when he is actually striking his head has moved out of line.

Some batsmen have been particularly unlucky in the number of times that they get hit when hooking. Bill Edrich, of Middlesex and England, was one. He got hit by Frank Tyson one day at Lord's and was taken off to hospital, having lost a lot of blood. But he did not lose courage and he came back later that day to continue his innings. Bill, who must be getting on for fifty now, still plays for Norfolk in minor county cricket, and my guess is that he is still hooking.

John Hampshire of Yorkshire is among the present school of batsmen who enjoys hooking, although within twelve months he has suffered three nasty head injuries. One was in the field, but another was against the bowling of Charlie Griffith in 1963, and another on the mat in Bermuda in 1964. I do not know whether this will cause John to eliminate the hook, but I think he has the courage to carry on especially if he makes sure that he gets inside the line as he plays the shot.

In the middle of your swing—to get

The cut. The back foot has gone across to the pitch of the ball, taking the head and eyes with it. The weight is on that back foot, and the bat chops down and across the line of the ball, with the head following it all the way

back to practical advice—you roll your wrists over, making sure that as you strike, the face of the bat is facing mainly down towards the ground. This ensures that you won't be caught at long leg.

The pull is another 'in-form' stroke. Played to a straight, but very short ball, it is aimed at mid-wicket, and again the old

formula comes in. Into line, swing across, turning the wrists as the ball is hit, and you will rap the pickets very firmly if everything is right.

The leg glances, forward and back, are very useful shots these days. The in-swingers and off-spinners that are so often around the place make it vital that you should play them properly.

It is important not to 'flick' at the ball on your legs. The shot is out of control, and you are inviting the attentions of some short-leg 'sharks' if you are not over the top of the ball, more or less in the defensive positions. Top hand dictating, bottom hand relaxed, keep the bat straight, and the ball will slide down and probably through the close fielders for a comfortable single.

The sweep takes a great deal of practice, as the bat is at right angles to the ball's line as it comes at you. A well-pitched-up ball just outside the leg stump is the one for this, and your first move must be to shove your front foot exactly towards the ball.

These pictures show the full follow-through of the cut, either fine or square of the wicket

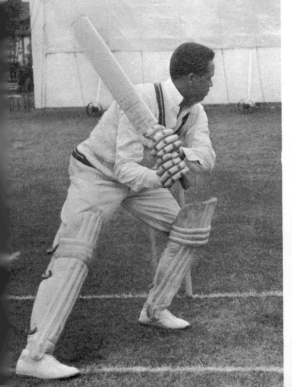

A lot of people sweep with their front foot straight down the pitch, but this clearly invites anybody to clean bowl you round your legs. Again, the wrists roll over to keep the ball down near the ground, but perfect selection and timing are essential to make a safe success of this shot. Do not try it unless you have played it well in the nets, and then only when you are feeling in 'real good nick'.

One of the most amazing sweepers, I suppose, was Denis Compton, who occasionally hit it so late that it scuttled past long stop for four. This needed such an exact combination of selection, daring and timing that we would all hesitate to try and teach it to a young player just trying to find his way. I am equally certain Denis was never taught how to do it. He just tried it out in the nets, found it working well, and promptly got away with it marvellously in first-class and Test cricket. It began to get him out later in his career a few times, but the devastating effect it had on top-class bowlers was well worth the risks he took when younger. Once he swept so late the ball went an inch wide of his OFF stump, and beyond the astonished wicketkeeper for four!

This was a classic case of a player building up his own technique out of one that was basically sound anyway. In much the same way, you will find no coaches at all trying to teach the leg hit as Rohan Kanhai does. This is a fantastic shot, often played with both feet in the air, but he has made it profitable. Kanhai is so strong; he is small but has the framework of a weight lifter.

More orthodox, but a similar example comes from Peter May. The way he used his forearms and wrists to whip a good length straight ball wide of mid-on was often baffling in its power and effectiveness.

All these players have found that their particular gifts and preferences have allowed them to develop something special in the way of attacking shots. But notice this well—it has all been built on to a firm, solid foundation of position, balance and 'watching the ball'.

As I have tried to emphasise, there is a lot more to batting than just playing strokes. Batting is run-making, and run-making is putting together all the bits of ability, taste and choice that make up batting technique.

Running between wickets is a very neglected art, especially in club and school cricket. The simple fact of the matter is that fast, intelligent running between wickets can bring you two or three runs an over without needing to make the attacking shots that carry with them an element of danger.

Always run fast, that's a fundamental. Always back up from the bowler's end, and be on the alert for a run. Always call firmly and decisively. There are three calls, and three only, although some seasoned players have worked out their own methods. The basic calls are 'Wait', 'Yes' or 'No'—making sure you only use one at a time.

Calling is the basis for good running, and although the time-honoured rule is a good one, I do not agree with it completely. The old saying was that if the ball goes behind square of the wicket, the non-striker calls; in front of the wicket, the striker calls. In the case of an edged shot behind the wicket, I agree. But if the striker has played a good shot, and his eyes are following the ball, I say he is the better man to call for strokes behind the wicket.

What you have to remember is that no wicket is worth surrendering for a run. If there is any doubt the call is 'No'.

Only if both players are of the same mind, and decided on a run is there one there.

If you are called for a run, go hard for it, and only in the very extreme circumstance send your partner back. If you do not do it quickly, do not do it at all, just go as hard as you can.

If the ball is in the outfield, run just as hard. A simple misfield in the country can be an easy two if you take the first one well, and furthermore, it can fluster the fielder into a bad throw for one more, or even earn some overthrows.

When making your ground at the other end, stretch your bat out as far as you can, and slide it in over the crease as you get in. Obviously, this reduces the time you are spending out of your ground.

Get a firm understanding with your partner about which side of the pitch you are going to run on. Quite a lot of run-outs are caused by both batsmen watching the ball and colliding stupidly in the middle of the pitch. You can grab quite a few more runs by some intelligent co-operation as you are passing on the pitch. For example, ' Have a look for three ', or ' Watch it, he's a good thrower ', can be very useful information between the wickets. Experience will teach you which is the ' danger end ' and usually, the man running to the danger end will decide whether or not that final run can be taken.

Experience will teach you how to handle a situation when you are running out of partners, or are trying to shield a new batsman from a particular bowler. You have to be pretty well set yourself before you can do this sort of thing, but you can do your team a power of good by using your own good form and ability to make things easier for your partners.

Here again, you must use your own judgment of a situation, coupled, of course, with any instructions your captain may send out. He may be angling for a declaration, or a chance to put in his hitters when the fast bowlers go off, but do not be put entirely off your game.

Getting on with some fast scoring does not mean slogging at every ball and getting out an over and a half later. That is no earthly use to your team if you are the man in. If you get out, it probably means that a fresh player has to swing at the ball, without your recent experience of the conditions, and this may start a great collapse that could lose you the game.

It is all a matter of situation and experience, but you must always remember that cricket is a team game first and foremost. You must always have that in the back of your mind. If winning the game depends on your getting out, you must do it, and let someone with perhaps different talents have a go. Also, do not let the business of reaching fifty or a hundred affect your outlook on the game. I know it is difficult, especially in club games, but the needs of the side must always come first.

I shall never forget some wise words once muttered by that great Australian Test bowler, Bill O'Reilly, who said, " Cricket is a batsman's game." From the crowd's point of view, and basically, it is, but this simply makes the challenge to a bowler more interesting and exciting. After all, there can be no batsmen without bowlers.

CHAPTER THREE

BOWLING

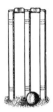

Y ou may be able to bowl the fastest ball in the world, the most vicious leg cutter, the quickest leg break or the most deceptive googly, but it will be no good to you if you have no command of length and direction. This you will only get from continuous hard work in practice, intelligently applied and thoughtfully worked out. You may say that you have seen many good batsmen removed by full tosses, long hops or simple straight balls, but I shall immediately counter by saying that these were only successful because they were produced—often by design—in the middle of long, accurate spells of bowling of any type, and that the bowler had his adversary in such a defensive state of mind that when the 'bad' one came along, it was such a surprise that it caught the batsman unawares. He tried to hit it too hard or in the wrong direction, forgot some of his basic technique, and paid the penalty.

Here is one thing to remember. Do not be an automatic bowler. Always have something up your sleeve by way of variety. A slightly slower one, a quicker one or anything else, and you can only achieve accuracy with these specials by practice.

Charlie Palmer, who came to the West Indies in 1953/54 as M.C.C.'s player manager, who was a cultured batsman first with Worcestershire and then Leicestershire, was also a handy medium-paced bowler who liked to experiment with a donkey-drop delivery. This was a ball released with a high trajectory and aimed at landing on top of the bails. I am sure that he bowled it a lot in the nets to make it accurate and he used it sparingly in the middle as an element of surprise. He certainly caught us napping when West Indies played against Leicestershire in 1957. He got Rohan Kanhai out with such a ball and Frank Worrell, laughing his head off, said, ' Fancy falling for one like that.' A few minutes later a chastened Worrell was making his way back to the pavilion. He had been the fall guy for exactly the same device.

Palmer was one of those cricketers who

35

played in spectacles. There was a theory at one time, of course, that while a bowler might get away with wearing spectacles in first-class cricket (e.g. Bill Bowes), a batsman would never reach the top. In recent seasons, however, there have been some fine bespectacled batsmen. Mike Smith, who has captained England, and Geoff Boycott are two English players who have made the grade, while Eddie Barlow of South Africa was remarkably successful in Australia in 1963/64. I doubt whether any touring batsman since Wally Hammond, with or without spectacles, has been as successful, which defies the theory that in Australia's sunshine, glasses are a handicap.

Barlow is one of those batsmen who does not believe in lucky and unlucky patches. He thinks you have to go out into the middle and make your own luck. Perhaps there is something in this. In his double century against Australia at Adelaide, he flashed time and again outside the off stump and time and again he edged over the slips. He must have made sixty or seventy runs this way, but the point was that when he flashed the bat he flashed it hard, thus ensuring that the snicks went at a great rate.

In first-class and Test cricket, bowlers win matches much more often than batsmen. There is much more of a balance in one-day, and afternoon cricket, when time is limited, but still the bowler begins with the initiative. In the first place it is up to him to bowl at the batsman.

You can theorise until the small hours about bowling techniques, and I hold the view that too much of this is done. Many a ' natural ' bowler has been stuffed up so much with bowling theory that he tends to lose a great deal of his natural ability, which largely means his action deteriorates in the search for something new, and he finds he cannot get anyone out.

This, as always, is the acid test. If you are getting people out, carry on in your own sweet way. If you are not, you will have to do some thinking.

As with all phases of cricket, there is a firm basis to sound bowling technique which can be applied to most players in the effort to make them better than they are. As usual, too, there are classic exceptions to the generally accepted beliefs, which appear to destroy them.

This, however, is not so. One of the greatest leg spinners ever, they say, was Clarrie Grimmett, the Australian. His round-arm bowling, however, contravenes most of the bowling theories we hold today. Ray Lindwall, one of the greatest fast bowlers, bowled with his arm a good deal lower than the upright position which is generally regarded as a prerequisite of class.

Curious that these were two Australians, but not so curious really when you think that their wickets are beauties, and that English coaches had not got to work in those days. Nevertheless, for every top-class bowler who does not fit into the right groove, you will find scores that do. In fact, the exceptions became great despite their ' faults ' rather than because of them.

At this point, I think it wise to have a general word about cricket coaching in broad outline rather than in close detail, especially as bowling is the most difficult item to teach anyway.

To me, coaching comes in two distinct phases. First, there is the beginner stage where the coach has to do his utmost to capture the pupil's interest in the game. He must try to make it understandable, and not the terrible mystery that some like to portray. He will pick up very simple items and by concentrating on

Ted Dexter misses the outswinger. Edgbaston, 1963

eradicating mistakes, and substituting sound schemes, he will put over the idea that the game is not impossibly difficult to learn.

Two very simple examples come to mind. You will find a lot of young batsmen trying to swing every ball away to the legside. Naturally, they will miss a lot. Line up a dozen balls between wicket and wicket, touching each other. Invite your youngster to swing across that line as he has been doing in the net. He will disturb only three or four. Ask him to push straight down the line, and he will disturb the lot. Then gently throw a few straight ones at him, and get him playing every one instead of missing.

Again, many youngsters find it difficult to bowl straight overarm. Get them rocking their arms at full stretch sideways for a time, and when they are acquiring the idea, have them stand at the wicket with the ball in their hands. At last, tell them to let go at the right time, and they will find the ball going a good deal straighter than before.

These are very simple, basic things, but if you get the youngster to feel he can solve them, you have gone some way towards establishing his interest in the game. If he spends half an hour missing everything bowled at him, then finds himself unable to get any of his bowling anywhere near the stumps, he is quite likely to chuck it up and go off to join the nearest cycling club or beat group. I think, particularly in England, more very young players are lost to this sort of thing, by the wrong sort of sympathetic treatment, than to anything else.

Your job as a coach relies on getting the interest of the complete beginners, and goes on until they are fairly useful club performers.

Here is the most difficult part of coaching. A simple tip about the position of the feet or head can often work wonders for a young player, but it does need very careful observation before you say a word.

Certainly, good coaches are born, and too many poor ones, I'm afraid, are made. The coach has to decide at what stage true technique has got to be observed without too much infringement on natural ability. This is the really critical test of a good coach, deciding at what stage he must alter a player's natural ability for the game.

This applies more in bowling than in anything else, because we all bowl just a little bit differently. In fact, however, most of the successful bowlers of all types do conform to a set pattern of action, at the vital point of delivery. Above all, the great bowlers have immaculate control of length and direction, and are always ' trying something '. They are never automatic. They are also perfectly balanced, have a free, easy run-up, and make the maximum use of that run-up. They waste none of their effort.

The position at the point of delivery is the one that really matters. The classic action demands that the back foot lands parallel to the return crease. At this time, the front arm reaches high up in front, the head is level, looking over the front shoulder, and the back is arched.

As the arms whirl round, the front foot lands at the end of a stiff front leg, acting as the pivot of the action. The front arm cuts down straight to the side of the front thigh.

The chest is kept hidden from the batsman until the very last moment, then the arm swings through, brushing either thigh, according to which swing you are trying to impart. At the instant the ball is released, the arm is as perpendicular as you can make it, the head and eyes are fixed on the target spot on the pitch.

Your follow-through begins after the ball has gone, but you still watch the batsman, and end your run smoothly a good while after the ball has gone. That follow-through makes a world of difference to both the pace and the spin you have been able to get on the ball.

This is what we call a ' good action ', and it applies to most sorts of bowling, making allowances for the different positions of the wrist, and of feet on the return crease.

If you do it properly, it is a strenuous effort. That is one of the tests of getting it right! The upright arm gives much more control over direction, and also ensures that any movement you get in the air or off the pitch is not merely correcting the faults given by an arm that slopes down at about two o'clock when the ball is released. It also ensures that the ball is more likely to travel towards the batsman with the seam upright. This means that it is likely to swing more, and later, and that it is much more likely to change direction when one side of the seam bites into the pitch.

Some of the main errors in pace bowlers occur through being ' open-chested ' at point of delivery to the batsman.

This can start with the back foot wrongly placed, pointing more or less straight down the pitch. It carries on with the head studying the batsman from inside his front arm, instead of outside.

This takes the bowling arm way down below perpendicular, and while it often adds to pace, it usually means poor direction and loss of late swing in the air. On good wickets against good batsmen, only the very extremes of pace are likely to be at all effective if the action is poor.

The idea of the ' sideways on ' delivery with the head looking over the front shoulder, is largely designed to bowl the dangerous outswinger. This is the one likely to get your best batsman out, especially if it goes late. Your lesser player, however, is more likely to play and miss it!

He is likely to be a candidate for the inswinger, which is much easier for a right-arm bowler to produce, as it does not really demand such a good action. Nearly everyone can rush up, and with a fairly high arm and reasonable position of the feet, produce some sort of inswinger. It is well to remember that an inaccurate inswinger is meat and drink to a batsman, and a sore problem to the captain and especially his close-in legside fielders.

Bowling, as well as batting, can be improved by ' shadowing ' as I call it. Go through the motions in front of a long mirror in slow motion, and you can often pick up and attend to your slight errors.

With pace bowling of all sorts, much depends on how you hold the ball. It is held lightly, in the finger-tips, and not clamped in the hand. Normally a right-hander will space out his first two fingers each side of the seam, and support the ball comfortably with his thumb underneath, at the side of the seam. I know of one regular hundred-wickets-a-year-pacer in county cricket who could never swing the ball with this grip, no matter what position the seam occupied. A wise old cricketer told him to place his thumb directly under the seam, instead of alongside. Straight away, the ball began to swoop about, and, if you try it out, you will find that this seam position helps towards getting your bowling arm higher.

My own grip for bowling seamers is not quite orthodox. I have pointed out that normally the bowler will space out his first two fingers each side of the seam.

Left (above) : The start of run-up for the seamer. Ball set in hand, right hand concealing position of seam in fingers. Eyes on target spot on pitch

Centre : Slowly working up to full running pace, head kept still, eyes on target, concentrating hard

Right : Last but one stride before delivery. Back foot about to land parallel with the crease. Right arm reaching up 'to pick the apple'. Looking over shoulder, which is pointing at first slip (to a right-hander)

40

The moment before delivery. Right arm reaches up. Still looking at target over shoulder. Back arched to get maximum leverage. Front foot about to be braced to form pivot for the swing of shoulders and arm. At this moment, the batsman should not see any of the bowler's chest at all. Front foot will land facing cover

Extreme left : Just after the ball has gone. Full weight has gone to front foot. A loose wrist has uncocked and the important follow-through has started

Right : Follow-through continues smoothly, and my expression suggests it wasn't a bad 'un !

41

You will see from the photographs of my own action that I keep my own first two fingers close together. Here is another example of variations on the orthodox methods being employed best to suit the individual.

Normally, and given a good action, the ball will follow the way you slant the seam. It points to the slips for the outer, and leg slip for the inner. Following through with the bowling arm either side of your leading thigh also helps either movement, but never try to ' put the ball ' there. It is rarely much good if it swings all the way, which often happens when you put it there. Any player worth his salt can counter this easily. It is the late swing on a well-pitched-up ball that first attracts the forcing forward shot, then gets the edge.

Some medium-paced bowlers have also developed the trick of the leg cutter and off cutter. As often as not, they come as the result of a good action with a slight turn of the wrists, at the time of delivery. They can, of course, be bowled by design, but they often tend to upset the rhythm of the basic action if bowled too often. However, as in all this, the young player will want to experiment for himself. The leg cutter comes from putting the second finger along the seam, and at the moment of delivery sliding it across, so that the ball rotates anti-clockwise towards the batsman in the way of a leg break. The off cutter comes similarly, but the other way around as the first finger rests on, then drags across, the seam.

Most youngsters want to bowl fast at first. The thrill of the flying stumps, and the feeling that your mates are afraid of you is really something, and shows an aggressive streak that you must have to get to the top in any sort of sport. Never discourage a lad who wants to be a fast bowler, but help him to become one. Do not let him overdo it, either by striving for pace at all costs, or bowling too long at a stretch. He will need real fitness, physical strength, a philosophical outlook, exceptionally strong shoulders, back and behind, and healthy feet if he is to succeed. Given all these, and the will, he might make it. Help him all you can, because the fast bowler always attracts the crowd. The game could do with more men like Wes Hall and Freddie Trueman to bring a spice and character to the game.

Spin bowling of all sorts is a fascinating art. The blast and the physical challenge of the fast bowler gives way to the artful scheming that plays on the mind every bit as much as the technical ability to bat.

I was an orthodox, slow left-arm bowler at school, and bowled round the wicket as most do in England. Mainly in Australia they bowl over the wicket, hoping to angle the ball away into the slips. I still preferred to bowl at or outside the off stump, with a quicker one coming into the stumps as a variant. Pitches there are so true, as opposed to many in England, that you have to learn a few tricks of the trade early in life or get clobbered around the park!

I did not spin the ball much, being more of a ' roller ', but by varying my angle of delivery and changing pace, I picked up a few wickets and enjoyed chasing around the outfield. In those days, games in Barbados were played over three Saturdays, and I often played in two matches at once. If I got an early innings in one match, I would run 600 yards down the road in the hope of getting another innings in a second game, and do both lots of fielding. I sometimes got into a tangle trying this, but did not someone tell me once that Ranjitsinhji played in two matches at the same time

.ooking sideways at a seamer's grip. The loose wrist indi-ates that more whip is being looked for, and that a bouncer : quite possible. Finger-tips rest lightly on ball, not grip-ping it tightly. Thumb is on bottom of seam

when he was at Cambridge and made hundreds in both?

Luck can play a decisive part in cricket, but you have to turn it to your own advantage. I was fortunate to have a trial game in Barbados in 1952/53 and get in the side against the Indians. I had been selected as twelfth man for the match, and was very unlikely to play until pace bowler Frank King was picked for the Test and rested from the Colony match. I took seven wickets, and the next year, helped Denis Atkinson to put on over a hundred against M.C.C. This helped to get me into the final Test of that exciting series, and although we lost it (levelling the series 2–2) I had a lucky break. Sir Leonard Hutton and Trevor Bailey had put on 155, then I had Trevor caught behind in my first over. That match gave me four wickets, a few runs, and an interesting little talk with Denis Compton.

Another view of the orthodox seam grip, with thumb slightly to one side of seam, and top fingers slightly apart

He looked at my fingers, suggested that they were too short to allow me to become a real hard finger spinner, and wondered if I had ever tried the chinaman or googly method of wrist spinning. I bore it in mind, and as a variant to the orthodox in English League cricket, I decided to ' give it a go ', and experiment by bowling out of the back of the hand.

A lot of practice and encouragement from my captains gave me heart and confidence to try it in the middle, and eventually I found myself with another string to my bow. It was especially useful in India in 1958/59, where we normally had plenty of runs to play with, and my captain, Gerry Alexander, reckoned that I would be effective if I landed two out of six properly. He proved right, an example of how hard practice and sensibly practical captaincy can increase your capabilities as a player.

Spin bowling, then, has had many moments of triumph in every grade of cricket. At the moment, English county cricket suffers from a lack of them simply because the wickets are rougher, and offer

Orthodox slow left-arm round the wicket, turning the ball from leg to off at a right-handed batsman. The arm must be high, and the front shoulder facing the batsman to ensure maximum spin from shoulders and fingers

Another view of same delivery. Head steady, concentrating on target, weight just moving on to front foot

The chinaman, an off-break to a right-hand batsman. This is the unnatural spinner, opposed to the natural finger spin. The b... comes from the back of the hand, with ... thumb out of the way, and full impetus giv... through the back, the shoulder, and m... important the wrist. The wrist is cocked j... before releasing the ball as hard as you c... Note that arm and shoulder positions are s... as before—the basic essentials

44

more dividends to bowlers of medium pace and above. These generally give fewer attacking opportunities, and the game as a spectacle suffers very much in consequence. The England Test side suffers in much the same way when it has to perform in the normally good batting conditions offered by Australia, India, South Africa and West Indies.

The finger spinner is the more conventional, the right-hander bowling off spinners, and the left-hander normal leg spinners turning away from the right-hander.

Ideally for this, you need long, strong fingers, with hard skin. For the grip, rest the ball on the table, seam up. Then extend your first and second fingers as far as you can. Slide them down the seam, then let the ball nestle on the skin just where the fingers join the hand. The real purchase for the spin comes from your first finger, and you will see why most spinners of this type get corns, or

This time the wrist goes right over the top, and with the ball spinning from leg to off (to a right-hander) we have the googly. The effort of turning the wrist right over at the top of the action tends to make the front shoulder drop. It is difficult, but try to eradicate this, as it can give away your googly, or 'bosie' as the Aussies call it

hard callouses on the top joint of this finger. This type of delivery is much easier to control than the unorthodox wrist spinner, but will get you a great deal of turn on dusty or drying pitches of the ' sticky ' type.

Jim Laker, the masterly off spin bowler of the fifties, had fine big fingers for his spinning job, but he still had to give the ball a real tweak to gain the results he was able to achieve. Constantly spinning the ball off his index finger created its own occupational hazard. The knuckle joint of Jim's right index finger became just about twice the size of that on the other hand. This has developed because of hard work and arthritis set into the joint. Towards the end of his career Laker found he could not play six days a week because of the pain the arthritic joint caused him but, of course, his overall record made the sacrifice worth while.

I have known our own off spinner, Lance Gibbs, spin the ball so hard that blood has literally dripped from his fingertips. He has gone on bowling. This is the sort of spirit, of course, you need to reach the top in any international sport.

The grip for the leg spinner or left-hander's chinaman is similar. Here, however, three fingers rest on the seam. The first and second are much nearer together, and there is a wide gap between the second and the third. This is the one that exerts the pressure, and provides the turn. The wrist provides the flick, and the third finger provides the ' kick ' of this one. The ball comes out of the side of the hand, spinning a great deal harder than the normal finger spinner, although both actions are designed so that the seam will bite on the pitch to give it maximum pace and turn off the pitch.

The googly is a development of the leg spinner. In this, at the moment of

45

delivery, the wrist, instead of (for a right-hander) facing mid-off, is turned right over facing mid-on. The ball comes from the back of the hand, spinning in the opposite direction from that of the leg spinner or chinaman. If all this sounds terribly complicated, a look at the photos will explain it. The top spinner, a very useful ball if you can perfect it, is a sort of halfway house between the leg spinner and the googly, the ball being released as the seam spins straight up and over towards the batsman, giving it increased pace off the pitch, and proving an excellent trap for the man expecting the googly. A top spinner, in effect, is a straight ball, and it is surprising how many good wickets in the highest form of cricket are gained with the straight 'un.

All these spins can be best started on by using a tennis ball, bowled underhand. The googly in particular is easy to do in this way, and trying the other spins will give you a good idea of what type suits you best. Once more, I say, have a go at this, that and the other, the more you know about how things are done, and the various problems of doing them, the more you will appreciate seeing them done superlatively well.

In very general terms, it is a crime to bowl short to anyone. This gives the batsman a splendid chance of summing up what the pitch and the bowler are doing, and gives him plenty of time to watch and deal with the ball bouncing a long way down the pitch. Unless you are trying something special, keep the ball well up to the bat. The batsman has less chance to alter his mind when you have made him play forward, particularly when you have committed him to his drive, with full power.

If the pitch is wet and slow, the slow bowlers will have to pitch the ball up farther, as anything just a little bit short can easily be dealt with off the back foot. Also, he will want to bowl a shade quicker, in order to counter the slowness of the pitch.

When the ball is turning a lot, or sharply, the spinner will change his ' line ' to make sure of giving himself the maximum opportunity of hitting the stumps, and making the batsman play the ball. For example, with the ball turning a lot it is a waste of time the left-hander bowling at the off stump, where the alert batsman can leave it alone. He needs to bowl at leg stump. The same applies the other way around to the off spinner. In either case, it is often a good idea to change your line of approach from over or round the wicket. My answer to all these complex considerations is work it out, do not be afraid to change either your line of fire, or your field, and when you have found the right way, stick to it.

If someone starts to hand you a bit of hammer, do not just bowl faster and wider. Try a few a good deal slower, with a slightly different field placing, and never be afraid to experiment by giving away a few runs to get a valuable wicket. You need a steady, sensible outlook to be a good spinner, and furthermore, you need an understanding captain to get the best results.

You will find that spin bowlers can be very effective indeed in school and club cricket. Most bowlers in these games are medium paced, and seeing the ball up in the air, apparently begging to be hit, can be the downfall of many a heavy scorer, especially if you offer a spinner to him early in his innings.

Also, not many batsmen these days are prepared to use their feet properly, and even if they do go down the pitch, they are quite likely to try a real ' windy woof '

Left : Try this grip for the off-cutter. Fingers together this time on the seam, thumb placed the side of the seam you expect the ball to follow after hitting the ground

Right : Leg cutter, with thumb on other side of seam, fingers still together at top

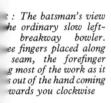

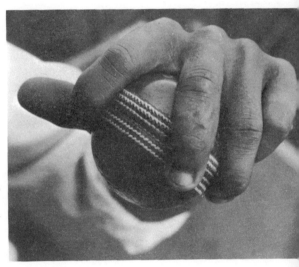

t : The batsman's view ...he ordinary slow left- ...breakway bowler. ...ee fingers placed along ...seam, the forefinger ...g most of the work as it ...s out of the hand coming ...wards you clockwise

...t : Overhead view of ...chinaman grip. Three ...rs still on the seam but ...the third finger does ...work spinning the ball ...from off to leg

Left : The back view of the chinaman, show-ing how the ball will spin from left to right of the picture

Right : The back view of the googly. The grip is the same as for the chinaman, but the wrist rolls right over, completely changing the direction of spin. This one will turn from right to left of the picture after it has left us

47

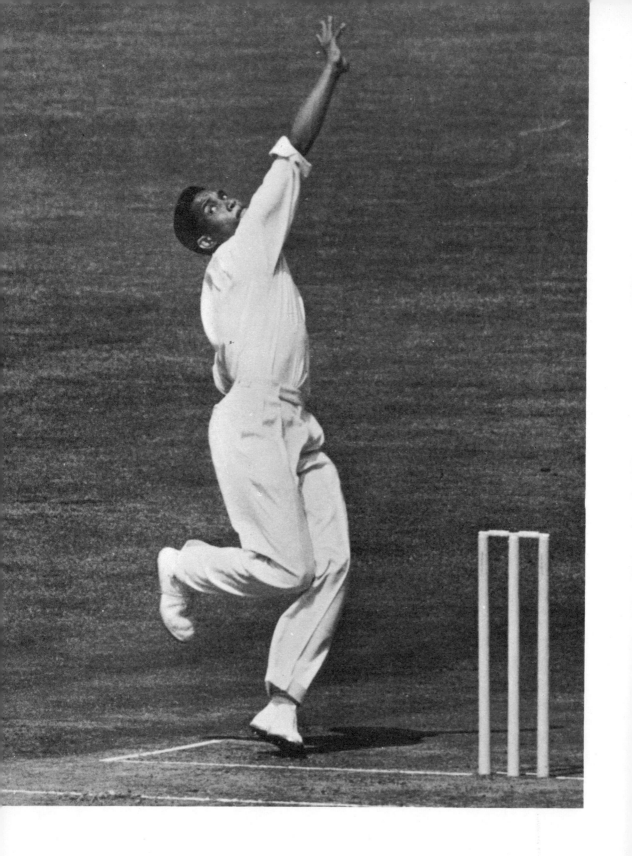

Plenty of effort going in before the ball leaves . . .

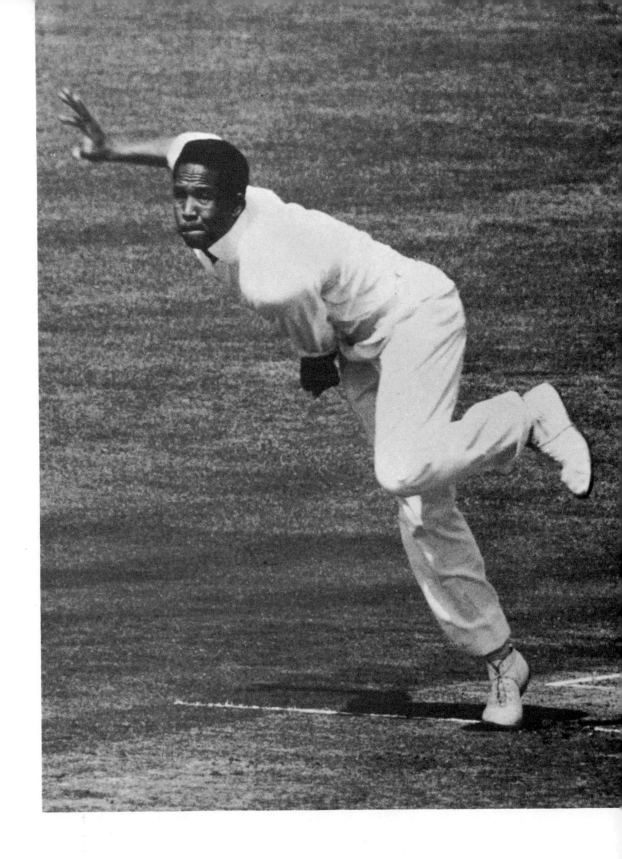

. . . and after it has gone.   The Oval, 1963

if they find they are not quite in the right position.

Wrist spinners especially are often very useful against firm-footed tail-enders, who can 'push down the line' till the cows come home against the seam bowlers. In fact a friend of mine, captaining a club side, got so many tail-enders out with his variable leg spinners and googlies one season, that his team-mates began to call him 'myxamatosis' (the disease that accounted for so many rabbits).

Still, a ball that gets a wicket has done its job, no matter what it is, and recalling my earlier story about Charlie Palmer never be afraid to try a full toss or a long hop, especially against a new player struggling to establish his innings. He can quite easily try to hit too hard, and miss it, or wallop an easy catch in the outfield. It counts just as much as a really fizzing leg cutter which pitches on the leg stump and flicks away the off bail.

In short, it's in the book! And as Freddie Trueman once muttered on bowling a Number 11 with such a trimmer, " That were a beauty, wasted on thee! "

The matter of tactics and field-placing are largely the captain's affair, but of course the bowler is intimately concerned.

The points of real danger for a new batsman are when he first gets in, when there is a quick fall of wickets at the other end, and he has to take over the batting for his side, when he is near fifty, and when he is approaching his century. In each of these cases, the bowlers must put maximum pressure on the batsman, and your quick bowlers in particular will always save a little extra effort for a new batsman, to catch him when he's fresh. Pressure can be built up by extra bowling effort, and by 'crowding' the bat with a few extra close fieldsmen. This game is played as much in the mind as by the body, and few enough club, school and, indeed, first-class captains seem to realise this.

Think about the game, try to put yourself in the batsman's shoes, working out his hopes and ambitions, and you have gone a good way to solving the way to get him out.

Bowling is a fascinating, elusive art, and as with any other phase of the game, you can never stop learning about it. By practice, done intelligently, and observation, done astutely, you can often come up with several answers to your main problem, that of getting wickets as quickly as possible in the minimum time there is.

If you have the skill, the action, the variety and the stamina you can, of course, bang away all afternoon with reasonably satisfying results. But if you combine all this with the ability to pick weaknesses and strengths, likes and dislikes, and guessing at probable reactions to different situations, you will find cricket is far more than just a pleasant form of physical exercise.

How right was the lady, who, fairly new to the game, overheard some crusty old professors going deeply into the whys and wherefores of a recently concluded match and said, " Cricket? It sounds more to me like chess played with a hard ball." This is it, almost exactly. But much, much more exciting.

CHAPTER FOUR

FIELDING

UNLESS you are going to be the greatest genius the game has ever known, playing for the best side of all time, you are going to spend more of your cricketing time fielding than doing anything else.

This simple fact alone should be enough to convince every cricketer that he ought to make himself as good a fielder as he possibly can. In doing it, he will get far more enjoyment out of his game. After all, you always enjoy doing something that you can do really well, in which you can take a real pride.

In adding to his own enjoyment by being a good fielder, the young cricketer also makes life a tremendous lot easier for his bowlers, captain and batsmen. This often gets forgotten, especially in club cricket.

I think that one of the reasons is that no genuine figures can be kept about fielding. You can count how many catches a chap takes, but there are never any statistics kept on how many half-chances he does not go for, or how many runs he allows by slack or shoddy work in the field.

If you care to think about it, you will agree that fielding plays a vital part in any set of bowling or batting figures, but, unfortunately, this is hidden from the normal view, which does not see exactly what has happened every time.

A bad slip fielder, for example, can cost his side a lot of runs in the first few overs, but if he goes in and makes a century, that is the fact that is remembered and taken account of in the averages.

In round figures, he has cost his side, say, fifty runs, but how can you measure exactly in runs and time what he has cost his team in the disappointment to his bowlers, exasperation to his captain and overall encouragement to his opponents?

Bobbie Simpson, of course, is now established as one of the world's great cricketers. He is captain of Australia and one of the most prolific batsmen of his era. He is also a more than useful leg break bowler. But it was as a fielder that Simpson won his recognition first in Test cricket. Bobbie fields beautifully

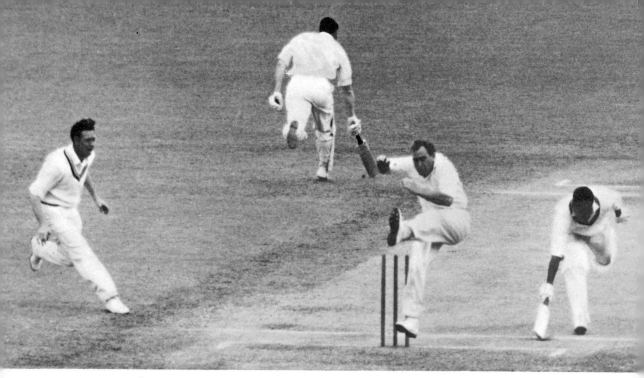

Bags of action here. Ray Illingworth jumps out of the way as Brian Statham's direct throw hits the wickets and runs me out for 99.
South Australia v M.C.C., Adelaide, 1962

One that got away. Basil Butcher drops a sharp slip chance off me.
Brian Close is batting. Edgbaston, 1963

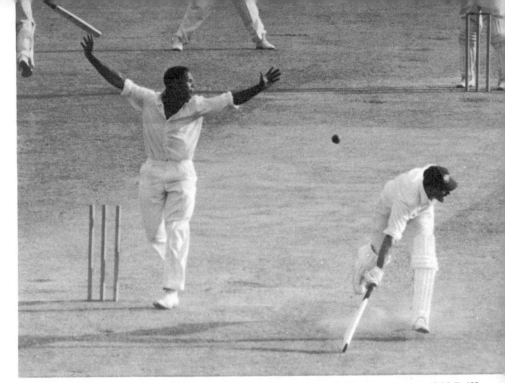

Backing up again, I have a shout (unsuccessful) to run out O'Neill.
Sydney, 1961

I was glad this one stuck.   Catching Neil Harvey right-handed in the gully.
Brisbane, 1960

anywhere, but it is at slip where he has achieved a reputation second to none. He is equally brilliant taking the fast snicks off the quick bowlers, and the edges, deflection and slashes off the spinners. Simpson has been known to drop catches, of course; he would not be human otherwise. But he catches many that others would not even get a hand to, and it is his anticipation as much as the sureness of his catching ability that would make him an automatic choice, together with his other attributes, for any World XI of the present day.

Just to make the thing crystal clear, I will drum up a simple imaginary situation in a club match, and show what a vast difference can be made simply by fielding well.

Batsman Jones has just arrived at the crease, and slow left-hander Smith is bowling to a fairly defensive field on a good pitch. Jones quietly pushes back a couple of maidens just to see what's going on as far as pitch, light and bowlers are concerned. When he's feeling a little settled, he launches into a few cover drives to test his form and reflexes for the day.

A fumble in the covers gets him off the mark, then a couple more bits of careless movement and covering give him two more boundaries. Mr. Jones is feeling pretty good, and realises that he can wait for his scoring chances and take them as they come. Also, bowler Smith reckons that he's got to do something pretty well on his own even to quieten down the scoring. To get a wicket he's got to do something a shade sensational. Consequently, he tries to do something extravagant, produces a bad 'un, and friend Jones whacks it out of sight. The batsman has been allowed to get into business as the boss.

Now, supposing Jones had come in under slightly different circumstances. He plays his first couple of overs steadily, then begins to put more power into his strokes. A couple of cover drives that he really middled are brilliantly stopped in the covers. Looking for a quick single, he has to scamper back in a great hurry as cover point comes racing in to change his mind.

After a while, he might reasonably be wondering when his first run is coming, and where from. He decides that when the chance comes, he will either have to try to push one through the onside field, or hit one over the top of the ' vultures ' in the covers.

Bowler Smith's mind is working along these lines too. He throws up one a bit higher and wider, Jones has a rush of blood to the ears, and forgets for a second all about that perfect cover drive he's been playing so well this season. He fails to get to the pitch, lunges to reach the ball, and pops up a little dolly to extra cover.

The bowler and fielder get their names on the card, and rightly too, but there is no space in the score book to pay tribute to the brilliant cover fielding of the previous twenty minutes which led directly to the dismissal.

The moral is obvious. If you go in against a side that is prepared to dive around the place to save a run, hurtle full length to try for a quarter-chance, and is quick enough to make most singles a big hazard, you realise two things. First you will have to hit the ball mighty hard to get any runs, or second, in some very unusual directions. This gives the bowler a terrific advantage, and the best sort of encouragement. Further it gives him and the captain the confidence to experiment towards getting quick wickets, and it is the fielding side that is calling the tune.

…ave moved to the line of the ball as quickly possible, and got my body behind it. Head d eyes are still, concentrating on getting is bouncing ball into my hands. The main ight is on my back foot, ready to transfer it to the front foot for the throw.

The ideal position for the pick-up, with the ball taken close to the toe-cap. Everything is right for the quick transfer of weight from back to front foot during throw, and I'm looking for a run-out if anyone tries to take two to third man

This is a bit of 'blocking' fielding. A firm hit to mid-on or mid-off can be stopped this way, but don't try it from the outfield. The knee is too low, and the position too cramped to get in a quick throw

In the first case I mentioned, the batsman realises that he can build up a steady, secure beginning without the slightest risk, taking the odd single here and there, and just waiting for the bad ball. He's a different player.

Anyone with a bit of ' ball sense ' can make himself a reliable fielder. The positions close to the bat need extra special gifts of eyesight, concentration and anticipation, but out away from there, anyone can make himself into a safe stopper, catcher and reasonable thrower. Usually it pays to let a chap field where he is happiest, but very often in club cricket you'll find that that is the ' quiet ' place, and not necessarily where he is of best use to his side.

It is a good idea in club teams to give every one of your players a chance at each position. Even if it does not suddenly produce a battery of wonderful short legs and slip fielders, it gives some of those who like to hide away on the fence a chance to ' get into the game '.

If your fast bowler complains about the number of slip catches that have gone down, it is often a good scheme to let him have a go at it, just to experience the problems and extra nervous tension of fielding close up.

Good fielding, like anything else worth while, starts with hard work. It is a more natural thing than either bowling or batting, and the rewards of hard, enjoyable practice are quicker to see. As I have said, anyone with a small basis of ' ball sense ' can make himself into a reliable fielder and, gradually, practice will build up the confidence to do the right things in the field without even thinking about them.

In time, you will find that in stopping the ball, and picking it up, you unconsciously put yourself into the right position for a quick throw to round off a competent piece of fielding. Experience will tell you very quickly that there is no point in moving until you have sighted the ball properly.

55

The throw. Eyes on target, shoulder and front arm acting as guide to the throw. Weight coming forward to front foot (top left and centre)

Right : Arm, shoulder and back have all lent a part to the final act of throwing, with weight all on front foot. Note eyes and head still concentrating on target, which is top of stumps. Full follow-through brings power and accuracy to the throw, but not quite as much as a stack of practice!

As with all things in this great game of ours, position and balance are all-important. When fielding, always do your best to get head and eyes facing along the line of the ball as quickly as you can. Always get your body well behind the ball to make sure you stop it, with something even if not your hands. When you are retrieving from the deep field, make every effort to get to the ball in such a way that your throwing arm picks it up, and that your weight can be quickly transferred for the throw. The aim, of course, is to get the ball back to your 'keeper in the fastest possible time. It all helps to build up the pressure on the batsman.

There are quite a few basic principles to this critical part of the cricket scene, which I will go into a little later, but always remember that in making your own fielding better, you will increase your own enjoyment tremendously, make your contribution to the game more important, and perhaps, best of all, please the spectators.

Even if they do not know much about batting and bowling techniques, anyone around the boundary recognises, and thrills to, a fine piece of fielding.

Furthermore, by using your intelligence in the field, you can make life a great deal easier for your bowlers and captains. Try to work out what's going on, and what your part in it is exactly. Move about the place as if you mean it, and when there's a left-hander in, do not just wander about the paddock looking lost, waiting for the captain to show you where to go.

Always watch your captain carefully. He might want you to move a few yards to match some special scheme of his which might work better if the batsman does not notice particularly. Of course, I do not mean close fielders moving when

the bowler is running up. That is rightly frowned upon as unfair tactics.

When you get a chance, watch the top-class people in action. See how they slot into their places, and move even when the ball is not coming to them. See how the close fielders stand, and notice what they do when the ball is coming. As a leg slip or short leg I like to stand as close as possible. I wear a box for extra protection and am surprised more close fielders do not take this protector normally associated only with batsmen and wicketkeepers. Incidentally I've heard of one Canadian wicketkeeper in Calgary who uses a baseball catcher's face-guard for extra protection!

Pay attention to what the older cricketers say, listen, and sort it all out for yourself. I have always been a great listener—it always pays. Watch your more experienced players, and you will usually find that what suits them will be best for you too.

But this is not necessarily so. Think it out for yourself, and if you think you 'have something' that they have not told you, or have put differently, try it out yourself. Rules of thumb at cricket can be very useful indeed, but by intelligent practice and trial you will often find something that fits your special talents and choices a good deal better than the generally accepted ways of performing.

I am a great believer in trying things for yourself. Do not just accept that 'this is right' and 'that is wrong'. Go off quietly and work it out. If your modifications still make sense, try them out. If they work, stick to them. It's results that count.

One good exercise for the fielder (and for that matter, the captain!) is to ask himself, 'Why have I been put here?'

Close fielders are there, obviously, to

catch, although sometimes a captain might set up seven or eight close fielders as ' propaganda ' to put the bite on a new player, and make him think batting is a lot more difficult against this side than it really is.

Bad starters particularly are apt to be unsettled by this sort of thing and goaded into an unwise shot very early on.

Most of the others in the field will be defensive, in the sense that they are saving one run. They must be agile enough to stop the hard hit, and quick enough to stop the sharp single for the gently played defensive stroke. Your boundary fielders are there to stop fours, turn the difficult two into a run out, and take the high catches. These things, of course, are by no means inflexible. Different bowlers will have different ideas about how to get different batsmen out, or cut off their supply of runs, and adjustments will have to be made.

But it all forms part of a proper pattern, a real scheme towards winning the game, not a pleasant and convenient way to fill up time until the tea interval.

By interesting yourself in this pattern, and applying intelligent observation to the simple facts you see, you can make the whole thing much more absorbing and enjoyable. You can also increase your own contribution to your side's effort, and as you gain experience at ' reading a game ' you might even reach the stage when you can make suggestions to your bowlers and captain. If they are wise, they will either tell you where you are wrong, or try out what you have suggested.

One of the real truths about fielding is that a side which can push three or four balls an over away from the pitch for a single against slow or badly positioned infielders is scoring at well over a run a minute, without taking any chances. This is one of the things that fielding and field-placing is all about.

' What am I in this position for ? ' is an excellent question for any cricketer to ask himself. A good question deserves a sensible answer, and this can give a much clearer picture when you are trying to understand the game.

There's no point in being hide-bound about it, and, naturally, different situations demand different, but sensible answers.

For instance, on a normal dry and fast outfield, the boundary fielders must stay ' on the edge '. It is always easy to run in for the ball, but very difficult to run back.

If, however, the pitch and field are very wet and slow, you will find that the lofted shots don't reach the edge, and that the ball travels very much more slowly over the damp grass. So you will move in ten or fifteen yards, having sorted out the exact reasons for doing it.

Circumstances of game, pitch and out-field always change tactics, and by using your cricket sense you can counter them to the great benefit of your side.

Another important part of the fielding pattern is ' backing up '. This is really in two parts. When the ball is out in the country, someone must back up the wicketkeeper in case of a bad throw. It is no use standing close to him, because anything that beats him is also going to beat you. Stand ten or fifteen yards behind him, in line with the thrower, and on the alert to pick up anything that passes your 'keeper.

The other sort of backing up is at the bowler's end, when your bowler has completed the important follow-through of his action, and is in no position to run out anyone trying a quick one. If you are at mid-off or mid-on, it is your job to get to the stumps as quickly as possible to try for the run out or to stop any direct shies

Alan Smith, Ray Illingworth, not to mention G. Sobers registering different emotions just after Ray has dropped a difficult return catch. South Australia v M.C.C., Adelaide, 1962

at the bowler's stumps. In any case, someone else ought to have moved in to back you up as well. Seeing this in action gives a businesslike appearance to the cricket and, once more, puts that little bit more pressure on the batsman.

Nothing is quite so upsetting to a fielding side than to see easy singles being taken, or overthrows given away. When a man has a genuine chance to run out a player with a quick throw, even though there is no-one guarding the stumps, he is justified in having a shot. If it goes adrift, there is something wrong with the rest of the side's fielding arrangements.

Joe Solomon, of course, achieved immortality when at the crucial period of the Brisbane tie in 1960/61, he twice hit

A high catch. Sight it first, move underneath, then concentrate. Eye on ball until you can read the maker's name. Balance carefully. Hands chin high, slightly away from body

I reckon this is 'out'. Hands are brought into body, forming a firm, but relaxed cup for the ball. Don't receive the ball tensely, it may bounce out. Let it come, and 'ride' it a little as it comes into your hands

the stumps with direct throws. After that, of course, he simply had to be known as ' Dead Eye Joe '. Pulling his leg in the dressing-room afterwards, Ken Mackay said " Why don't they give you a turn at the bowling crease more often. After all you are the best chucker of the lot." The atmosphere in that dressing-room at the end of the game was unforgettable. Solomon's second throw, of course, ended the game with the scores level. He had to hit the stumps because there was no time for wicketkeeper Alexander to get up to them to gather the ball and then break the wicket before the batsman

made safe his ground. I was nearer to the stumps when they got hit, but I could not have achieved a run out. It had to be a direct hit. Kanhai was also close to the stumps when they were broken, and I suppose the picture of he and I leaping skywards is one of the best known now in any cricket library. Rohan was so excited he still thought we had won the match when we got back to the dressing-room. " We have done it, we have done it," he kept shouting, and only when Richie Benaud persuaded him that the scores were in fact level, was he convinced it was a tie.

I think Richie was a bit disappointed at the time that Australia had not pulled it off, which was natural for a captain with a side in the strong position they were ten minutes before the finish, but he, like everyone else, quickly came round to the view that it was the greatest match in which they had played. Sir Donald Bradman said it was the greatest he had ever seen. In that last over so many things happened and they have been described in such detail that I do not want to repeat them here, but there was a classic example of the bowler Wes Hall crashing into Kanhai when the latter was in a better position to take the catch. This was understandable in the white-hot heat of the moment. I think Frank Worrell called out Kanhai's name, but in the general hubbub Wes could not have heard.

Tom Graveney tells a story against himself as captain of Gloucestershire when a ball was skied into the covers and he shouted out the name 'Dave'. The ball dropped safely to earth to the relief of the batsman. Tom had forgotten that he had three players called David in his team. . . .

When a high catch goes up in range of more than one fielder, the captain will normally call out who is to go for it. Sometimes the fielder himself is in a better position to judge than the captain, and in this case it is his job to call 'mine' as loudly as he can. In passing, it is considered ungentlemanly conduct for a batsman who has skied a ball high in the air to call out 'mine'!

In these conditions, the captain and/or umpire would have to take a very firm stand on affairs!

Above all in fielding, the thing to remember is that you must go for the faintest possibility of a catch. Of course,

if a side wants three to win with five wickets and one ball left of the match, you can achieve your object simply by stopping the ball, and not risk a boundary by going for the catch. Otherwise, in all cases, you must keep going and exert every energy towards catching it. Many times a season, one fantastic catch completely changes a game, and you must have that in mind all the time. One brilliant catch can bring new heart to your bowlers and introduce a new determination through the whole side. It is worth remembering.

You will soon forget the cleaner's bill if your wonderful diving catch has won the game.

Now to itemise a few tips for specialised fielding positions.

First slip and leg slip. In these positions you must watch the bowler and the ball all the way. The deviations off the edge of the bat are likely to be small, so you can follow them without much movement of your head and eyes. Stand with your legs comfortably apart, equally balanced, and not too far apart to prevent quick movement either way. Your hands must be relaxed and fingers pointing downwards, almost on the ground. It is easier to get up than get down and it is vital to stay down until you've seen the shot. Arms should be inside your knees, but stretching forward so that you can get at anything that goes to either side. Actually, when at leg slip, I watch the bat. This is a development that has come with experience.

Normally, in these two positions, one must not move until the ball is sighted properly. Again, I have found that experience allows me to anticipate a shot from leg slip and move as soon as I see it taking shape. This is, I must stress, a thing which comes from much observa-

Backing up to my own bowling, trying to run out Bobbie Simpson.
Melbourne, 1961

Moving forward to catch Norman O'Neill at backward short leg off Lance Gibbs. Head and eyes right on line. Melbourne, 1961

tion and experience of individual batsmen, and I would not recommend it as a starting principle for young players.

All the other slips and gully. They take similar positions as to feet, hands, etc., but watch the ball off the bat. The angle between the flight of the ball from the bowler and the movement of it from the bat is too great to watch the ball all the time, so you have to concentrate on picking up the ball as soon as it slides off the bat.

Short leg. This is a real specialist position which needs loads of experience, and a great deal of courage. Normally, club bowlers are rarely accurate enough to have them really close in the way first-class players can. You can usually tell what sort of shot a batsman is going to make by the position of his feet. If he is going to ' smear ' at, say, an off spinner, your forward short legs and short square legs take cover, that is, make sure they get out of the way. You cannot catch a really firm hit in those positions.

I do not duck, I shift position, trying to keep my eyes on the ball, or, if this is impossible, turn my back on it.

I think the first inkling I got of the effect a great short leg fielder can have on a game was in 1957, when Tony Lock was at his peak there. He was an education in short leg fielding behind the wicket.

As I say, you also need a great deal of courage, and also confidence in your bowlers, to stand very close. In club and school cricket, it is a bad mistake to stand too close when you are not used to it. Your inexperience will probably mean that you do not catch anyone out, and also you can get some nasty cracks up there. Nevertheless, it is an exciting challenge to anyone and can make a world of difference to your bowlers.

Cover point, mid-off, mid-on, mid-wicket. Move in towards the bat as the bowler is running up. This gets you mobile, and gives you a start as you swoop in to cut off a boundary or prevent a single. Never set full sail until you have seen and plotted where the ball is, then go as hard as you can.

Whenever possible, get some part of your body behind the line of the ball, to make sure it does not pass you, and always be on the alert for a run out. Hard, flat throws always speed the game up, and your practice periods should have given you the confidence to pick up and throw in one movement, with no time spent for the ' wind-up ' of the throwing arm, which makes all the difference between an easy single and a run out.

Long-on, long-off, long leg, third man, and other boundary fielders. Here you want your safest catchers and longest throwers. They must take great care to stay where they are put, and again, must never move until they sight the ball properly. They

will, as the covers do, be walking towards the batsman at the time the ball is delivered, but it is no good tearing hopefully off into the bush if you have not an idea where the ball has gone.

High catches are taken with the fingers spread but hands near together, and the ball meets them at about chin-high. There the ball is always in focus. As the ball comes, the shock of it will be absorbed by ' giving ' just a little as you form your hands into a cup to receive it. Let the ball close your hands, do not do it yourself before it arrives or you will get some unpleasant finger injuries.

Much the same applies to any other catches. It is important not to ' snatch ' but let the ball come naturally into your hands. Of course, you have to make yourself competent at these mechanics of the game long before you take part in a serious match. Do your best to be able to take catches with either hand, although if you possibly can, it is always safer to get both hands to the ball.

You will almost certainly be a better catcher with one hand than the other, but try to develop the weaker one. I believe it was the Arsenal soccer manager, Billy Wright, who had the right idea about this. When a youngster, he found that by far his best kicking foot was his right, and he tended to work the ball on to that foot. His first manager spotted this, and made him wear a light sandal on his right foot, so that he rapidly learned how to use his properly booted left.

For the reason I stated in the first sentence of this chapter, you've got to enjoy fielding. You must love to chuck a ball about and catch it from all angles and in any conditions. Try to bring variety and competition into your practice, and remember, the ball hit with the bat always gives the most lifelike practice.

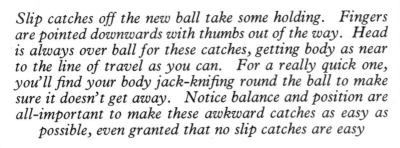

Slip catches off the new ball take some holding. Fingers are pointed downwards with thumbs out of the way. Head is always over ball for these catches, getting body as near to the line of travel as you can. For a really quick one, you'll find your body jack-knifing round the ball to make sure it doesn't get away. Notice balance and position are all-important to make these awkward catches as easy as possible, even granted that no slip catches are easy

Much of this comes back to personal fitness, and it is impossible to stress how important this is to the budding cricketer. You've to be loose, and supple, and attentive—all the things that build up from fitness. You feel better, and your performance will please you more.

I reckon that half an hour flat out at fielding training is far better than a long drawn-out series of things stretching over two hours. Make it brisk, competitive and entertaining, and it will be really worth while. Short matches on the middle are very good exercise, and you can learn a great deal about the game with practice matches of this sort. One good wheeze to get things moving is to have a rule that the batsman must run for every stroke. You will be surprised just how much he gets away with.

When I was a youngster, three of us used to line up in the covers and challenge the batsman to drive the ball through. This sort of competition adds life, meaning and value to something that can be a real chore if it is not properly organised. All the time this is going on, you might as well get used to throwing very simple catches to each other.

It is amazing to me how many people throw the ball back to their bowlers at a difficult catching height, making him stoop and, rightly, swear at this useless waste of valuable energy and patience. As any Australian Test player will point out, a fielder doing this to Wally Grout will soon be suffering from blistered ears.

All these little things add up to giving cricket a pattern and a rhythm which can be wonderful to take part in, and watch. Fielding, above all, pays off handsomely for the practice you put into it, in the delight and value you can get out of it.

The lightweight boots I find suit me best. I have always found a flat shoe more comfortable, so there is no built-up heel. For bowling, I have a steel cap around the toe. The lower top line to the boot prevents chaffing the ankles. I like the flexible kangaroo skin uppers and the green hide sole, and find them much less tiring than the ordinary boots

CHAPTER FIVE

WICKETKEEPING

As he is the most important fielder in the side, I am giving him a piece all of his own. Your wicketkeeper can make or mar a fielding performance more easily and quickly than anyone else in the side. Consequently, he needs, above all, to be really fit, both in mind and body because his is the most taxing job in the field, in both psychological and physical senses.

Once again, and I make no apology for repeating the fact, position and balance are essential to good wicketkeeping, even more so than in any other phase of the game.

I have had a short go at wicketkeeping, which taught me plenty, and also taught me that most of the established beliefs are the right ones. Although a lot of sides believe it, they do not always follow the rule, " Always play your best wicket-keeper." The Australians, however, always insist on the best 'keeper at all times and at Test and State level you will often find the 'keeper batting at number 11. A poor wicketkeeper can give away a lot more than he is ever likely to make, and his effect on a team can be devastating. More chances, especially early ones, go to him, and if he floors the first few you are struggling uphill.

Do not, if you can avoid it, pick a wicketkeeper just because he bats a bit. In the same way as a lot of alleged ' all-rounders ' get into sides, you will find that doing a bit of everything very often amounts to not enough of anything.

Anyone in a club who fancies a go at this difficult job should be given a good chance. You do not want to miss the slightest chance of capturing a really good stumper. They are hard to come by.

Keeping wicket clearly has a lot in common with batting. Your 'keeper must watch the ball as keenly as the batsman. Head and eyes must be kept in line and no movement made until you see what's happening.

Assume that the batsman is going to miss every ball, and get into position to stop every one.

Jubilant West Indies players throw their arms in the air as Gerry Alexander dismisses Burge (Australia) off Valentine in an Adelaide Test match

Your normal attitude as the bowler runs up will be squatting, in as comfortable position as you can manage, with your legs slightly apart, and your fingers facing downwards. The position of your feet would normally be spanning the distance between the middle stump and a few inches outside the off. As with the slips, always stay down until the last moment.

For an offside ball, you move your right foot out, but never backwards, to get your head into line. You let the ball come into your gloves, ' give ' a little to take the shock, and bring the ball back towards the stumps to give you the stumping position.

The legside is, of course, much more difficult, because you are blanketed by the batsman's body. Although it is very difficult, always try to watch the ball off the pitch, and move across, never backward, to get behind the ball. Instinct and actual play are the only ways to improve this difficult and most important part of the wicketkeeper's job. Except in extreme

Godfrey Evans (Kent and England) claims another victim

situations, always keep balance on both feet. You have to do this to make sure you are in position for a stumping, and, if you are, don't look at anything but the ball until it is safely in your hands. It is the umpire's job to look at the batsman's feet at the moment he misses the ball.

Sometimes it pays to hold the ball for a while, in case the batsman overbalances and gives you a chance to stump him.

One vital thing about standing back to the faster bowlers is to get right back. Standing halfway is hopeless. You will miss the snicks and obviously have no chance of stumping.

Most fast bowlers prefer to see their 'keepers back, as this makes the catches easier, but, of course, once more we have the great exceptions. One of them was Godfrey Evans and some of the amazing stumpings he took off Alec Bedser will be talked about as long as the game is played. Until you fancy yourself and your bowlers in this class, however, it is as well to start the easier way. Remember Godfrey could stand up to Alec (who preferred it any-way) because the bowler was so accurate.

The ideal place to be when standing back is just as the ball starts descending from its bounce off the pitch at the moment of receiving it.

You will quickly find out where the right place is after you have seen a few come off the pitch. It will vary, of course, with the pace of the bowlers and the pitch.

Although, in the course of their acti-vities, wicketkeepers can produce plenty of showmanship, this is absolutely no good if it is not supported by efficiency. You might see a chap dive full length to stop a wide legside ball. It might be necessary, but another, more competent 'keeper might well be able to get there in two quick steps, with head, eyes and balance perfect. Agility and fitness again.

Among the neatest of English 'keepers of my time has been Keith Andrew. It seems crazy he has represented his country only twice.

Your pads are there to protect your legs, not to stop the ball. Some club 'keepers I have seen wear enormous and cumbersome ' wicketkeeping ' pads, but in my view they just slow up movement, and give them the idea that the pads are a prime method of stopping the ball. Pads are protection both in stumping and batting, and should never be used as a first line of defence in either case.

Wicketkeeping equipment is obviously important. Inner gloves, usually of chamois leather, and slightly damped, are a good idea, and outers should be as good as you can afford. Make sure you have softened them up before match use, and never have either inner or outer pair of gloves too tight. You will some-times want to put a piece of extra protec-tion inside the gloves, such as tape, cotton wool or modelling clay, so there should be a little room. The old-timers even used beefsteak to protect their hands from bruising. Perhaps padding today is improved—or steak too dear!

You can also get oil to lubricate the palms of your outer gloves, but make sure it does not become sticky in the hot sun, getting the ball gluey and seriously handicapping your bowlers.

Everything your stumper does or does not do, is important to the game, and a great deal depends how he looks after the throws from his fielders. He can do a tremendous amount by moving around briskly, and really making an effort to clean up untidy throwing. If a wicket-keeper is lazy enough just to stand at the stumps, waving forlornly at a wide throw, plaintively whining, ' Back up,' you want to do two things.

Gerry Alexander leaves the umpire in no doubt !

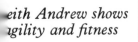

...eith Andrew shows ...gility and fitness

First, tick him off and let him know what effect his performance is having on the rest of the side, and secondly, find another wicketkeeper.

Furthermore, I have often noticed club sides walking out on to the pitch and seeming to think that good practice for your 'keeper is to stand about ten yards away and blaze the ball at him just as

Rohan Kanhai, an example of a player developing day by day (see Chapter 7)

hard as possible. I would say it is a good way to bruise his hands, and make them worse during the afternoon, besides the very real possibility that he will put down a couple by trying to take the ball in the undamaged part of his hands.

If your 'keeper does damage his hands during a match it is a good idea to have someone else standing by to do the job. Any further damage to your specialist 'keeper's hands could upset his confidence first, and keep him out of the game for an important few weeks.

A fit and efficient wicketkeeper will smarten up a whole side in the field. He will love to get fast, accurate returns over the top of the stumps from the field, even if no run is being attempted. Also, this sort of enthusiastic skill is never lost on the batsman, who realises he is pitting his wits against a team and not a rabble.

One thing about wicketkeeping that should attract more young chaps to it is that you are always ' in the game '. You are in the best position to see how bowlers are performing, what the pitch is doing and what frame of mind the batsman is in. Although your whole attention must be on the ball at the time it hits the pitch, your observations can be of considerable value to your bowlers and captain.

Wicketkeeper/captains can be an excellent idea providing they have the mental manoeuvrability to concentrate ferociously when the ball is in play, but relax into tactical thought and planning between balls and overs. Gerry Alexander did a fine job for West Indies in this capacity. He also showed a superb example in sportsmanship when he stood down in favour of Worrell and still backed him to the hilt.

The old principles hold good for your wicketkeeper. Watch the ball, get into line with it, do not snatch, and concentrate always on the balance and position. You will learn by long, but I trust, interesting spells of practice, and you will realise you are right at the heart of things.

Wes Hall in action during a Test match

Late swing beats Brian Close covering up, and finds him lbw. Edgbaston, 1963

*Ray Illingworth has played neither forward nor back to Lance Gibbs, and I dive
from short square leg to catch. Port of Spain, Trinidad, 1960*

CHAPTER SIX

CAPTAINCY

I HAVE never read a cricket report which begins, " Despite the brilliant captaincy of Jack Robinson, leading a very weak Dymchurch team, the powerful Rivertown side won the match on Saturday by two wickets."

Somehow, that sort of thing is never sought out for particular note, and it points the cricketing moral, unfortunately true, that in the public view there is no such thing as a good losing captain.

If, by clever changes of his fielding tactics, or a change in batting order which works out well, he wins the match, the public tends to give the credit to his bowlers, batsmen and even sometimes his fielders. If the same set of alterations have just failed to come off, and he has narrowly lost, the general view is that he should have stuck to the ordinary run of things and not tried all these fancy manipulations.

Unfortunately, that is the way it is, and a skipper in all types of cricket just simply has to live with it. Consequently, he has got to be a strong character, resilient in his outlook, prepared to gamble, and keep his finger right on the pulse of any game he is captaining. Furthermore, he has to be a sort of father-confessor, knowing all the likes and dislikes of his side, ready to chivvy or sympathise at just the right moment for best results, quick to seize any opportunity of taking charge of affairs, and always looking cheerful and hopeful in the most depressing of circumstances.

He must at all times be prepared to defend his moves, and his players from informed criticism, and be man enough to discount ill-informed criticism for the rubbish it so often is.

To get the full respect of his side, he must always be prepared to have a spirited go at anything he asks of any of his team members, and never let them feel he has lost interest, or is just waiting for something to turn up. At all times he must be utterly unselfish, prepared to sacrifice his own wicket, or the chance of getting some wickets, if he feels it will be better for his team in the long run. His job is not only

Neil Harvey again, this time at slip. Well-balanced, head on the line, hands just receiving it off Frank Worrell. Melbourne, 1961

to win matches if they can possibly be won, and avoid losing them if they cannot be won, but also to keep his team and officials happy. So often a captain can make a good, happy season by his personal example and spirit even if his side is losing a lot of games.

He must be a good sportsman, and diplomatic in his dealing both on and off the field; ready to take a firm line if he feels he is being taken advantage of, or generously conceding a point if he thinks it is in the interest of the game as a whole, and cricket in particular. In short, he has

a twenty-four hours a day job.

If he does a lot of good, constructive things for his team and cricket, it is probable, too, that he will make some honest mistakes. A long time ago, someone said that the man who never made a mistake never made anything, and this is so true of cricket captaincy. It also points to one absolutely firm fundamental about this—the most difficult thing in cricket. A captain can, and must, never stop learning about the game.

Every hour at practice, every match played in or watched, and any piece of

Roy Marshall, whose ability was very quickly recognised by Hampshire when he toured England in 1950

*Alan Davidson (Australia) bowling to Frank Worrell (West Indies)
in the Third Test at Sydney, 1961*

cricket talked about, can teach you something. Only a very unwise cricketer ever forgets this. Of course, the game is greater than any individual in it, and if this sounds like one of the old pious platitudes that get trotted out at every annual dinner, I make no apology for it. It is true, it is important, and everyone ought to have it in mind all the time.

First, you must play cricket hard. I can see no point at all in playing at half-cock. It reduces your pleasure in the game, and gives less value to any of the performances in it. Playing hard does not mean glowering at your opponents, appealing for ridiculous decisions, and being bad-tempered about the whole thing. Far from it.

You can be cheerful, light-hearted, sympathetic and courteous to your team and your opponents, but it still does not prevent you playing the game as it was meant to be played—hard and competitively.

In these days, there seems to be fewer born leaders of men, and leading a cricket team ought to be the same as captaining it, although in many cases it is not. Very often, activities off the field can point the difference between a leader and a captain. Your leader takes an active, although maybe quiet part in organising practice, team selection and possibly informal tactical talks, and, when the serious stuff is finished, he takes his full part in the social side of affairs.

This sort of respect, dating from his pleasant ability to lead, is far better than any discipline which is imposed by the letter of club rules, or etiquette, or, honestly, things that don't come from the heart.

79

*Tom Graveney, the anchor man in Worcestershire's
Championship success in 1964*

I fail to get on top of my cut against Shackleton in the Third Test at Edgbaston, 1963. Phil Sharpe is the catcher

I have been very lucky in some of my captains.

The best was Sir Frank Worrell, whose beautiful batting had dazzled and fascinated me since the time I was six years old. In captaincy it was not only that he was more experienced than anyone else I have known. He used his experience to build on the sound cricket sense he had already acquired, in much the same way as a batsman adds his own special strokes on to the basic requirements of run-getting to become a really top-class player. Frank knew all aspects of cricket and

cricketers, and you always felt he was ' thinking the game '. He used all his team's abilities according to what he felt was right, and adjusted his tactics to suit the various circumstances of every game. He was always working out ways of dealing with opponents, and was quick to spot any technical defect in their play. A case in point was at Leeds in 1963, at a time when Wes Hall bowled at his top pace. Frank noticed that Micky Stewart, the England opener, did not move his pads outside the line of the off-stump when leaving the ball. Coupled with his high back-lift, this gave the idea that one coming from the off into him would get him between bat and pad. He thought that Micky would be vulnerable to my in-swinger rather than Wes's greater speed. So he had a quiet word with Wes and gave me the new ball. To the great delight of us all, I got Micky in the first over.

Often, bowlers are exerting themselves so much, that they miss small, but important things like this. It gives them terrific encouragement if their captains can help them, and makes them think the captain's a wizard if it comes off!

Frank always kept very much in touch with his bowlers. He would always be asking, "How are you feeling?", and was always letting you know just what was going on. It was always comforting to know that the captain had a real grip on things, and was not just aimlessly swopping the bowlers and fielders around because he could not think of anything much else to do. Even if you are at a loss as to how to handle the side, you must never let them realise it!

I played for South Australia under Les Favell, another good captain. He was always game to 'give it a go' and, furthermore, he was always prepared to lead it himself, with some of the most daring opening batting I have ever seen. A good skipper will always take part in things himself. One who says, 'Come on, chaps', is a much better proposition than one who stands back and says, 'Go on, fellows'.

One of the best international skippers was Richie Benaud, who played it fair and very hard, as it should be played. He was totally absorbed in and by the game. Sometimes, I felt, he was a bit too emotional about things, but I do not think that ever upset his judgment of a situation.

Often, an emotional skipper gives his side the feeling that he is anxious and on edge. Richie's judgment was always sure, however, and he was also a born gambler, prepared to take the calculated risk. Best of all, though, I like the Worrell way. His calmness and imperturbability, I felt, gave him a chance to see and observe the game more and, sometimes, to cool down some of us when we started to get a bit too excited. Repeatedly in the mounting crises of the Brisbane and Lord's Tests he commanded, "Keep it cool, boys; keep cool."

All this makes it sound as though a cricket captain has got to have the nerve of a gambler, the poise of a financier, the human understanding of a psychologist, ten years more cricket knowledge than he can ever possess, and the patience of a saint. Ideally he has, but let's be practical and hope for the best. If you are a captain, you can do no more than your

Alec Bedser bowling in a Test match against Australia

best. But make sure it is your absolute best you are doing!

Your first job is to win the toss. In matches longer than two days, it is usual to bat. In shorter matches, when the wicket is unlikely to deteriorate much, you will often find it easier to come from behind to win.

It is not possible, however, to state definitely whether or not you should bat when you win the toss. It depends so much on weather, state of pitch, your own strengths and weaknesses, and those of the opposition, that you cannot possibly set down any fixed rules about it. Indeed, there are very few fixed rules about captaincy, fewer even than in the rest of the cricket picture.

I am often amused to read that it was a ' good toss to lose '. This means that the winner of the toss thinks it would be a good idea to bat, but that he is not too sure there won't be some hidden life in the pitch. It leads me to the view that there are not any good tosses to lose, but only captains who have not got the courage of their own convictions.

A knowledge of pitches and how they behave is a matter of experience and observation. I have known skippers win the toss on what they think is a wet pudding of a pitch, too slow for anything, but which turns out to be wet on top of a hard foundation, and a real ' flier '.

If you can stick your thumb in a longish way, it is usually too soft and wet to be dangerous. If not, you are better off bowling, bearing in mind that any side that is put in has it in the back of the mind that the opposing skipper really knows a thing or two about pitches. If you put the other side in, you must support this by really attacking. This will add to the idea that your bowlers are going to get something out of the wicket,

even if they fail to. There's a lot of ' kidding ' in cricket, and as your understanding of the game improves, you will see how it applies.

I seem to remember an England *v.* Australia match in 1956 when the Aussie bowlers, sensing the pitch was a dream for spinners, and that their batsmen would have no chance against Laker and Lock, just bowled straight, kidding England that the pitch was easy. By the time it was easy, they started trying to get England out again, realising that their own batsmen had an even chance. Such things as this are pretty advanced, and can lead to some great mistakes, but they are worth while bearing in mind when you are captaining any sort of side.

Any young man aiming to be a captain ought to make a point of having a look at every pitch he can, working out how he thinks it will play, then comparing it with what really happens. He must keep in mind the quality of the bowling and batting, of course, but observation and intelligence over a period of many pitches and years will help him when he comes to making his own decisions. Remember, too, that deciding how a pitch will play, especially in England, is only a shrewd guess. You can never be absolutely certain.

I have known many experienced English players foxed by our West Indian pitches. They can rarely read a pitch until they have played a lot there, and appearances can be very misleading. It points to the truth that when you are playing in a strange country or in a higher grade of cricket, you have simply got to feel your way, seeing, observing and listening to what is going on around you.

It is a captain's job to pin up his batting order in the dressing-room. Start with a fixed order at the beginning of the season,

Richie Benaud (Australia) bowling in a Test match against England at Lord's

but when form or injury leads to changes, make sure the person involved in the changes is the first to know. A quiet word before the match, explaining the circumstances can save the upsetting experience of reading about a change in the dressing-room or even in a newspaper.

There are plenty of things to be con-sidered in making up the batting order. It is often a good thing to have a left-handed opener. They can upset the bowler by making him change his 'line' for the two openers. Most of the time, your number 3 is the best player in the team, who can go in and establish an innings after losing an opener in the first

83

over, or play shots and dominate when the first wicket has fallen at 100.

Even when chasing quick runs, you must have a decent start to the innings, so you will always use your normal openers. Thereafter, you will be able to afford a few wickets as you put your forcing players in higher up, and save a couple of ' blockers ' if you get into a real tangle towards the end.

Let your players know what is ' on '. You will have to take decisions even though you are not in the middle, and here again you must know your men. Some players, when told to get on with it, are inclined to have a glorious slog as soon as they arrive, without regard to their responsibilities to the team.

Sometimes a quick twenty from a slogger can come in very handy, but remember that if it changes your mind from playing for a draw to going for a win, your opposing captain might well have ' fed ' those runs for that very purpose. In due course, you will probably find yourself doing the same sort of thing when you are in the field.

Especially in one-day games, a fine balance has to be struck between runs, wickets and minutes whether you are bowling or batting. This comes with experience, and conditions. Obviously, on a good wicket with a fast outfield, you may score 110 runs an hour. Yet sometimes scoring even 60 an hour can be a terrible problem. It depends on so many factors, that only experience can suggest to you how to deal with each situation as it crops up.

The opener of my time who had to take all that was flung at him was the Australian, Colin McDonald

Another of the captain's tricky responsibilities is declaring. Now let me say first, you declare with the idea of winning, and for no other reason. There is no point in declaring if you have no chance of winning. That's plain stupid. You declare because you think you can bowl out your opponents and win the game.

To carry on from there, you have to bowl to your declaration. If you have set a very steep task, and your opposition, by their batting, show they do not think it is feasible, you have got to get them interested. Here again, you may put on your ' muck ' bowlers for a while, giving them some cheap runs, but it is done with a real purpose . . . like dangling a carrot before a reluctant donkey.

When you reckon they are in the mood to go for the win, you will bring back at least one of your front-line bowlers to bowl them out. Now that you have them in a stroke-making mood, they have more chances of making runs, and you have more chance of them making fatal mistakes.

These are all fair, and good, cricket tactics. They are not contrived in any sense, because you have altered a position of stalemate to one from which either side has a chance to win. You have, as I have mentioned, ' dangled the carrot '.

Ordinarily, you will start your attack with two fast bowlers, if you have them, as they are more likely to make full use of the new ball. Sum up the pitch, and the wind, then make it an ' opening attack ', and not just a way of getting the game going. At no other time during the game will you have two entirely fresh batsmen at the crease and two entirely fresh bowlers. Make the most of it, and ' attack '.

If you feel your best chance of a wicket is using your slow bowler to open, why not? It is rarely done, but I have a notion that many first-class openers, and especially school and club players, would be more uneasy starting against slow bowlers than quickies.

As a captain, you should have made sure your bowlers loosened up a bit before going on the field, as nothing is more encouraging to an opening bat than to get off the mark in the first over with a couple of fours from long hops and full tosses.

Depending how the game is going, never be afraid to make bowling changes or to try bowlers at opposite ends to those from which they started. It is surprising how often in top-class cricket a bowler operates from the wrong end, through casual or even thoughtless captaincy.

Unless things are going very favourably indeed, never let the game just wander along comfortably. Study your opponents, how they stand, how they hold the bat, whether they are back or forward players and so on, and give your bowlers the benefit of your observations. If they cannot exploit them, try someone else. A change of ends, or changing which side of the wicket they are bowling from, can sometimes be as effective as putting on a new bowler. Remember how your bowlers, especially your fast bowlers, react to the game. A wicket or two early on will keep them going longer than if they are not successful, but don't keep them on so long that they cannot ' come back ' at any time to get at a new batsman or polish off the tail-enders.

Always encourage your players, and only in really bad cases of slackness or thoughtlessness, tick them off on the field. Occasionally, you will have to, but a word off the field is usually the pleasanter way to do it. If your bowlers, especially your slowies (and always be willing to ' buy ' a

'*Among the neatest of English 'keepers of my time has been Keith Andrew*'
(*see Chapter 5*)

86

Wes Hall, who brings character to the game

few wickets with them), cannot pitch a proper length, do not snarl at them, just rest them and give them a chance later on. In $99\frac{1}{2}\%$ of cases they are not trying to do badly, you know; everybody likes to be successful at the game they are playing!

The same goes for dropped catches. I say that the man who has never dropped a catch has not played very much cricket. Nobody drops them on purpose, and the chap who does feels a good deal worse about it than anyone else in the field.

Grit your teeth, bite back that sarcastic remark, and say, "Bad luck, George, you'll catch the next one." Very often he will.

A captain must, at all times, have a clear idea of what his bowlers are trying, and set the field in conjunction with them.

Many young bowlers will want to put a boundary fielder where a four has just been hit, and often they do get away with it. This is nearly always wrong, and happens because neither bowler nor captain has a real appreciation of what is going on. Assume, for example, your opening bowler is trying to bowl in-swingers. He will pitch the ball up and, quite possibly, get driven through the extra cover gap for four.

If the ball is swinging at all, now is the exactly wrong moment to take away one of the slips and put him at extra cover. An intelligent batsman will not try to drive when he sees it is going to be stopped. An intelligent bowler, however, will leave the field as it is, try to make one swing a little more, change his pace a shade, and the batsman, flushed with the pleasure of that cover drive, tries it again, finds he is not in the right place, is too far committed to change his shot, and is clean bowled between his bat and pad. This is bowling properly, and using the gaps in your field to bring the dangerous strokes out of the batsman.

You dispose your fielders to stop the runs and to take the catches. That much is obvious. But what is too often forgotten is that you use the gaps in your field to invite the dangerous, over-ambitious stroke which can get you a wicket. Your slow left-handers pack their offside fields to save runs, but also to make the batsman hit across the line of the ball to the legside, where there are not many fielders.

You cannot set a field to cope with a lot of bad balls as you have not got enough fielders. You set the field to cope with bowlers bowling reasonably well. It helps their confidence and gives your other fielders the idea that they are not just ' leather chasers ' but part of a variable, but sensible pattern for getting wickets.

You can perhaps afford to use one fielder to stop too many runs coming from the really bad ball. The obvious case is setting a deep square leg for the leg spinner, but there are very few others.

As a captain, you must keep an eye on the positions of your fielders (club cricketers are apt to wander a great deal, especially when the sunshine brings out the pretty frocks!) and always be thinking out ways of improving your chances of cutting down runs or getting wickets.

In England, on wet pitches, things can change almost from minute to minute. Indeed, I have seen wet pitches which, on a cloudy day, turn like wildfire when the sun is out, and next ball, when the sun is in, go as dead as a doornail, not turning or lifting the slightest bit. In these conditions, and in many others, you may have to experiment a great deal to find your ideal bowling and field-placing combination for the quickest results.

You may miss half an hour on a sticky wicket by using the wrong bowlers, when with the right ones, you might have 'copped' five or six of the best batsmen. It has happened, and it will happen again, but not to you if you are really on the ball.

One of the tests of your organising a fielding side is when you have say, numbers 1 and 9 in at the crease. Usually, you will be after getting them all out, and clearly you are more likely to get the rabbits out than the chap who has been in all the time.

Your class player will try and organise to get as much of the bowling as he can. You have to stop him, by changes in your field, and instructions to your bowlers and fielders. If you are really on top of your job, and your side is supporting you as they should have been taught, you will be able to stop the good player taking a single from the fourth ball onwards of the over and then taking the next over himself.

These tactical points can take on great importance at the testing time of a match, and these are the moments that sort out the differences between the men and the boys among cricket captains.

A club or school captain, of course, will have other duties to attend to. He will have to meet the opposition people, arrange about intervals, and possibly umpires and hours of play. He will also make sure that his side is decently turned out, with no fancy clothes or socks, and that they all have properly studded boots. It all helps the businesslike look of a team if they are clean and tidy too. Even if you cannot be a top-class cricketer, you can begin to look like one.

A club captain, especially, can do the game a great service by paying special attention to the younger, and newer recruits to his team. He should make them welcome, ask about their cricket, and have the information checked with other members of the club whose judgment he trusts. If at all possible, he should get these newcomers into the game and playing their part.

A lad who is persistently put in low down in the order often only gets in when either the order is 'swing for ten minutes before I declare', or 'hold out for a draw for the last twenty minutes'. He might only be given a couple of overs at relatively unimportant stages of the game.

Frequently, he will wear a path between mid-on and deep third man with not much to do and little variety to divert him and capture his attention.

Even if these things cannot be avoided sometimes, keep them in mind and don't establish a dull pattern for the youngsters who come into your team. Bearing in mind the requirements of the match, do your best to give them some responsibility in the game, and let them see that, young and inexperienced as they are, they have something to give you, and that you welcome anything they do give you. Encouragement in the early stages of a career is vital these days, but there is no need to go overboard and overdo the praise, because that will give a false impression too.

Honest praise and kindly encouragement can do a world of good in the early stages, as, indeed, can sincere criticism and understandable advice. Too many young people give up cricket because they find it too difficult, and because they do not 'get into the game' enough. Give them as much responsibility as you can, and always be ready with a cheerful remark and, particularly, a piece of praise and encouragement.

When you do give advice or criticism, make sure they understand what you are talking about, and exactly what you want them to do. Old cricketers have a way of talking that assumes that everyone else has access to the store of experience and knowledge they have built up themselves.

Do not fall into this trap, when you are trying to help.

Get them to ask you questions, no matter how silly they might seem, and do it in private if they are bashful about asking. Explain as simply and as carefully as you can. If you cannot explain, ask yourself why not, and go off and brush up your own cricket knowledge!

The fact that you are an experienced cricketer, with years of knowledge and practice behind you, having played hundreds of matches of all different sorts, gives you a privilege. As with all privilege, it also brings you a responsibility. That is to do your best to get your own love of the game into the others, probably the younger ones. You have enjoyed your cricket, so help somebody else to enjoy theirs. Again, by doing this, you will find yourself learning all the time, improving your understanding and appreciation of the game as you try and understand the problems of others.

Although it is nothing to do with captaincy in particular, I would like to add this: when you give up the game, take up committee work or umpiring or scoring, or helping with the ground, or something of the sort. When you were young, somebody helped in this way, and assisted at your pleasure. So do not just sit on the sidelines, moaning about present-day standards, do something yourself to improve them. It will keep you young for years after your playing days are gone.

First, it is a captain's job to win matches, and, if he cannot win, make sure that they are not lost. Secondly, he has to look after the overall discipline within the team, both on and off the field, earning their respect by personal example and a firm, sympathetic approach.

Thirdly, he must make sure that everyone enjoys playing with and against him. This means especially looking after the interests of new and young players. Fourthly, and perhaps most important of all, he must remember at all times that his school or club's name and honour is his own personal responsibility, all the time. Fifthly, that he has a mighty important duty to the greatest game in the world.

To do all this infallibly is perhaps impossible. To do it well is a triumph. To do it to the best of your ability is perhaps the best thing that can happen to a man of the right qualities.

I hope you will try it some day, and for a long time, too.

I feel it is appropriate to conclude this chapter on captaincy with the story of how I came to lead the West Indian Test players on to the field for the first time. It was the third game of the ' little series ', played between Sir Frank Worrell's team and various England XIs at the end of the 1964 season in the U.K.

Frank went out to toss and came back, announced what had happened, and then said, " Gary, you're in charge, you are skipper for this match." He did this so that I should have practical experience of leading the boys before I took charge in the series at home against Australia. It was a thoughtful and wonderful gesture which I appreciated, particularly as it was at Lord's. It was a great thrill to be O.C. for the first time at the headquarters of cricket. It was also a typically selfless gesture by Worrell, for this was obviously to be his last first-class appearance in a match in England.

CHAPTER SEVEN

SOBER REFLECTIONS:
Past, Present and Future

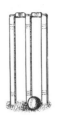

IN my opinion, there is too much complaining in cricket today, especially about bowling ' this sort of stuff ' and ' that sort of stuff '. Fast bowlers are accused of bowling too short; medium pacers of nagging at the leg stump; slow bowlers of packing their offside fields. At one time or another, nearly everyone is accused of throwing! I think that once you are on the field, there should be no complaints except with your own performance. If you want to moan, save it for the dressing-room, and pray it does not get into any book of memoirs!

I remember when I was seventeen I had first to face Freddie Trueman and he was wrapping them round my neck. I do not think I went down the wicket complaining. I took it as it came: I had been told this was the way, and I expect batsmen to follow the same line of reasoning.

Batsmen should be in the class to take what comes to them. The bat is there in the hands to provide all the answers.

The opener of my time who had to take all that was flung at him was the Austra-

lian, Colin McDonald. He was never much to look at, but he did his job magnificently. I never heard him complain, even though I suppose he ran into a bigger battery of real quick stuff from all the countries than anyone else. In his time England were richly stocked with fast bowlers like Trueman, Statham and Tyson; we had Wes Hall, Chester Watson and Frank King; and although I never saw them at the time, I have heard enough of the South Africans Peter Heine and Neil Adcock to suggest they were as quick as any.

Towards the end of his career McDonald took to wearing a waistcoat protector, as Colin Cowdrey did in the 1959/60 tour of West Indies. This was a sensible move against very fast bowling on rock-hard wickets and encouraged the batsmen not to flinch away.

I have always been particularly interested in opening batsmen, and one of the best of my time has been Hanif Mohammed of Pakistan. He is a very good player indeed, one who is never easily

ruffled, has a wonderful technique, quick reflexes and tremendous patience. If only his home wickets of Pakistan had been faster, he would have grown up to master his one weakness—against the really quick stuff.

In his methods, he is something like Len Hutton in that he is a slow player and waits for the runs to come. I did not see much of 'The Knight' in his prime, but he batted extremely well as captain in West Indies in 1953/54. He always dealt defensively with the good one, but never let the bad one get away. In his cricket technique and overall ability I found him very good to watch.

★   ★   ★

I sometimes wonder if cricket is being too greatly administered. It is excellent, of course, that so many willing and dedicated people should be prepared to work for the game long after their playing days are over, but I think many of their energies go in the wrong directions. I think they should be more concerned with fixture arrangements and ground and playing comforts than in jiggling about with the Laws. Far too many regulations have been changed even in my time. Most of them are aimed at making the game too easy for the batsman. I have not liked this front-foot law for the no-ball lately because it has curbed fast bowlers. The way things are going, they will eventually decree that a bowler's front foot will have to land behind the return crease, so that he has to bowl from about twenty-five yards. Experiments such as these could obliterate from the game such personalities as Hall and Trueman, because it would stop their successes. You can hardly be a personality without being a success. I would like to see a truce in experiments rather than a 'stop-go' towards new laws.

★   ★   ★

One bit of legislation I would like to see, however, concerns pad play. Far too often present-day players use their pads as a definite means of front-line defence rather than as protection for their legs. Even young lads coming into the game, are now padding off when they ought to be using their bats. An extension of this sort of thing could ruin batting as a spectacle.

That great stand of over 400 between Peter May and Colin Cowdrey at Edgbaston in 1957 had some of the lustre removed from it as far as I was concerned by this. Scores of times, they padded off—Cowdrey in particular—against Sonny Ramadhin, certain that no English umpire would give an l.b.w. decision on the front foot down the wicket.

A friend had an interesting experience on these lines back in 1959. He was watching Somerset play Kent on a turning wicket. The Kent opener, Arthur Phebey, a very accomplished player, was battling to save his side from defeat. Brian Langford, the off spinner, kept on bowling at his off stump and Phebey would take it on the pad, deliberately. He had had a knock in the previous match, and took so many more on the same knee that eventually it seized up on him, and he had to go off for treatment. Several wickets fell while he was off, but when he came back, his tactics changed abruptly. Now, instead of the pads, he began to use the bat with a real purpose, and ended with 77 not out, in a total of 173 all out. A good lesson if ever there was one.

★   ★   ★

Hanif Mohammed, a very good player indeed, one who is never ruffled, has a wonderful technique, quick reflexes and tremendous patience

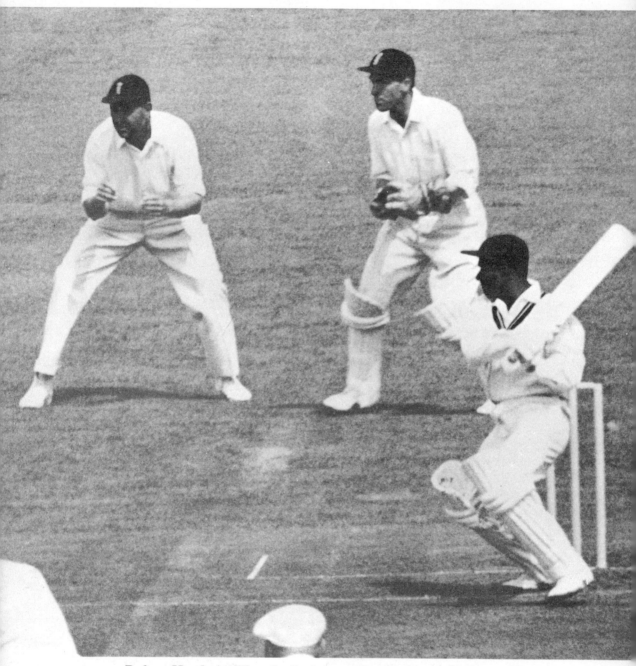

*Rohan Kanhai (West Indies) in action in the Manchester Test
against England in 1963*

*Godfrey Evans claims another victim under the
approving eyes of Trevor Bailey*

I should also like to see leg byes removed from the list of awards. It seems absurd to me that a batsman plays at the ball, is beaten by the bowler, the lucky deflection of the pad beats the field, and for all this rather feeble performance the batting side actually get a few runs for their trouble.

If leg byes were scrubbed altogether, there would be none of the confusion occasionally caused when umpires show different ways of deciding whether or not a shot has been played at the ball.

⋆   ⋆   ⋆

By the end of 1964, England had won only three of her last nine series, and had been beaten at home by Australia and West Indies. The papers have understandably been full of comment about it, and I should like to air my views.

I think they chop and change the England side too much.

One of the main reasons is that they have not settled on an established opening pair. They have been unlucky not to have found a new Hutton and Washbrook combination perhaps, but there have been too many compromise selections and not enough perseverance with players who have made the grade.

In 1964, John Edrich made 120 at Lord's—his first Test against Australia. He did not really fail at Leeds, but missed out in his one innings at Old Trafford, and then was left out of the Fifth Test and the M.C.C. party for South Africa.

In 1963, Brian Statham played in only two Tests against us, the First and the Fifth, when the pitches were perfect for batting. Yet he was the best fast bowler in England against us, and should have played all through. At least one result—

the Lord's Test—would have been different if he had.

I have often thought that a home team in Test matches would do well to name a Test squad of say, seventeen, just before the First Test and pick the sides from them for the first three Tests. It would be tough, perhaps, to some outside the seventeen and would not give any encouragement to others, but I think the germ of a good idea is there.

At least, I think that a player good enough to be picked for one Test ought to be picked for three in one series.

Still, 1964 was a funny season in England in many ways. With England's captain putting up for Parliament; Freddie Titmus opening the innings for England in the First Test; and Yorkshire having to play their scorer in the important Knock-Out match at Lord's, I suppose anything goes!

⋆   ⋆   ⋆

If I was lucky enough to play in a World XI against any other representative side, I would choose as my ground Kensington Oval—not to be confused with Kennington Oval. It is in Barbados, and the reason for my choice is that it has such a good, true batting wicket with enough bounce in it to help a bowler, and perfect sighting. There is a great wide screen there, and this cuts out all the business of 'gamesmanship' you can get with a screen that has to be altered every time a bowler changes his line of fire.

Most overseas grounds, with good light, naturally offer a clear sight of the ball, but in England, where the light is often very murky, efforts must be made to keep on improving the conditions, which means better backgrounds. This

*Tony Lock beats me with one that really 'bit' on the
broken turf at the Oval, Fifth Test 1957*

is where the administrators really can get working.

Lord's now has screens at each end, and I noticed at the Single Wicket Championship of 1964, it was easier to pick up the ball than in 1963. Previously, there was only a screen at the Nursery end, and I understand that the English batsmen still found Lance Gibbs, for example, tended to come ' over the top ' with his slower one. Another advantage with a high bowling arm!

Sight screens alone, however, are not enough. They have to be correctly positioned. The one at Manchester, for instance, was lifted several feet in 1964 because previously the ball often went out of clear vision over the top. At Sheffield against Yorkshire in 1963, the screen was so arranged that we lost sight of the ball under the screen! It was all very confusing, but I realise that the smaller English grounds have to use up all their available seating for big matches, often to the detriment of the sightscreen. I do feel, though, that Test matches should be played in the very best of conditions, if the players are expected to produce the best performances.

* * *

Six days a week county cricket often comes under fire. Some people think it should be cut down to week-ends. If this revolution took place, I do not know what would happen to first-class cricket in this country, because the players who make it up do live just for the game. Cricket six days a week has lasted a very long time, and played in the proper forthright way will continue to survive. Rising county memberships support this view.

The county game has established its traditions and should continue to live by them, although I can see a case for having a day in the mid-week off instead of Sunday, when a lot of people could come to watch. You will get your stale patches, but you will get your purple ones too, and the purple ones are worth waiting weeks to see. Alterations and constant changes are not good for the game. The players become confused, and do not know whether they are standing or sitting.

* * *

There is no doubt that running the Cup Competition alongside the County Championship provides a very entertaining variant for the spectators and I expect can be very enjoyable to play in. The important thing in these time-limit matches is that pitches should be good enough for one day, and not prepared to last for three days. Perhaps this will encourage teams to try and bowl each other out instead of simply clamping down on the runs. The weakness of the Cup at the moment is that you can win a match without getting a wicket.

* * *

I think it would be a good idea if overseas players could come into county cricket without upsetting their ability to play for their countries. If, perhaps, each county could offer one five-year contract, without a qualifying period, to one overseas player, satisfactory terms could be arranged to meet the requirements of player, club, country and most of all the paying public.

Think what such players as Bruce Dooland, Jock Livingston, George Tribe,

Len Hutton never let the bad one get away

Roy Marshall, Colin McCool, Bill Alley and their like have done for struggling clubs in the past ten years!

Roy Marshall has had a longer county career than any of the others I have mentioned. His ability was very quickly recognised by Hampshire when he toured England in 1950, when I think he was no more than twenty years of age. They were, therefore, able to get him at the right age and Roy, I suppose, did as much as any other and more than most—apart from Derek Shackleton—to make Hampshire such an improved side and to lead to their Championship success in 1961.

Here is another batsman who has succeeded wearing spectacles, and like Barlow he has pursued the idea that if you go for strokes outside the off stump you should really swing the bat. Too many batsmen get themselves caught in the slips through half-hearted prodding. Not so with Marshall. He lets the bat fly and the ball, of course, goes off it that much quicker. Roy provides an outstanding example of a player who has harnessed English and West Indian methods to the benefit of himself and the delight of the crowd. He has acquired a sound technique through his years of batting on English pitches and is a very good batsman against off spin bowling on a turner.

He has not forgotten, however, his Barbadian upbringing and still plays the joyous, free strokes of his youth. It seems to me that he has gained strength in England. He was always rather a lightweight in the heat of the West Indies, and perhaps the more temperate climate of Britain has suited him. Certainly there are many other overseas players who would adapt themselves quickly to England and make the first-class game

much more exciting for all and sundry.

One player who would pack the grounds is Rohan Kanhai. I have no hesitation in saying he has become the greatest batsman in the world today. One of the best-looking players, he is straight in defence, vigorous and brave in attack and has astonishing reactions. While he can play all the cricket strokes, he can play some highly improbable ones too. Some people think he is showing off when he plays that fabulous hook, finishing flat on his back. But it is the old story of where the ball goes that counts, and in Rohan's case it is a very long way.

He is an example of a player developing day by day, and increasing not only his ability, but also his concentration powers as he has matured.

*   *   *

Frank Worrell has a theory that in a batting line-up of, say, six specialists, one should not worry too much if there is a fifty per cent failure-rating per innings. His idea is that if even two and a half men come off the side is on its way to a good score. I would agree if he means by coming off they make hundreds and more. Brilliant fifties have their place but it is the hard-grafting 150 that turns a Test match. Remember if a match is scheduled for four or five days, the big innings win the matches.

*   *   *

I have heard it mentioned in England, and even in Australia, in the last season or so that with Benaud pulling out of the game, there is not the room there used to be for a leg spinner in top-class cricket. This is one of the most ridiculous assertions I have ever heard.

*One of the true 'greats', with whom I have been lucky enough to rub shoulders,
has been Sir Donald Bradman*

After 1956, Australia came back to the top because they had Benaud's leg breaks and Davidson bowling left arm over the wicket, leaving the right-handed batsman. The ideal ball for good batsmen is the one that leaves the bat. A good off spinner might hit the pads fifteen times in four overs without taking a wicket. The leg spinner beats the bat and leaves the pads. Providing he bowls on the right line, he must be penetrative. The thing is that leg spinning needs perseverance and plenty of encouragement. Saying that leg break bowling has no part in modern cricket is just about the most dangerous talk I have ever heard.

Top-class leg spinning against top-class batting presents one of the most fascinating sights in the game.

Benaud provides an example of the hard work that goes into it, and also the

Although it's a 'slowie', you can see that plenty of vigour has gone into this one. The Oval, 1963

fruits of such effort. The old saying that you do not get anything out if you do not put something into it was never more true. I did not see Richie between 1955 and 1960, but in that time he improved seventy-five per cent.

On his first tour of West Indies, he had good length, little turn, no googly and no 'flipper'. The years rolled by, and he improved out of sight. We found in Australia that he was still accurate, but now he had more spin, more bite and a well-concealed googly. He flighted the ball and used endless variety on an immaculate length. He used his head; he had experience and confidence, which dated from his hard work off the field.

Alan Davidson was a very great all-rounder and was successful in his bowling for rather the same reasons as Benaud. His best ball was his 'go away ball' which, bowled from over the wicket, did not need to do much, as it was already sloped towards the slips. You had to play at it in case it came in, and this combination of menace gave that fine wicketkeeper Wally Grout a great deal of his success. Many of his catches were from outside edges won by Davidson.

* * *

I find no difficulty switching from League to touring first-class cricket, because it is such a delight to get on the good wickets which are usually prepared for touring teams in England. Standards are different, but League wickets are so inferior, and it is very difficult to work out just what is happening to the ball. Joining Radcliffe in 1958 taught me a great deal about cricket in England. It was a lot different, and the fact that no runs or wickets meant less pay made me concentrate a lot more. I played the ball on its merits, and the League played an important part in developing my batting.

Against the counties, you can tell in a few overs how to read a bowler. For bowlers, the switch to much better pitches means less margin for error, but the fact of having first-class fielders makes the change easier. The average West Indies player enjoys his League cricket even if he sometimes misses the stimulus of playing regular first-class stuff.

*   *   *

I had an interesting experience in my season with South Australia in 1963/64. At first, I felt physically tired, after a strenuous tour in England. I have always believed in giving everything I had, but now I found I was forced to play within myself, especially as I had a lot of bowling to do as well. I cut out strokes that had previously seemed second nature to me. I found I had to 'pace' an innings carefully, and in the end it brought better results.

In 1964 the most prolific batsman in England was Tom Graveney. He was then in his thirty-eighth year. It should not be so surprising really that a senior batsman should be amongst the most successful. After all, Jack Hobbs made a century of centuries after he was forty. I do not think it is possible for teams today to carry so many veterans as in the past because of the more exacting fielding standards, but there is no doubt that when a player's legs begin to move less freely the extra wisdom he has accumulated can compensate. I feel that the case of Graveney in 1964 underlines the point. Tom was the anchor man in Worcestershire's championship success. He had all the old grace and ability but less of

Alan Davidson was a very great all-rounder

103

One of the best international captains was Richie Benaud (see Chapter 6)

the freshness of his youth. In playing within himself he was giving the bowlers less chance.

As a youngster, perhaps your brute strength and vigour keep you going, and it takes a lot of energy swinging the bat around and rushing up and down the pitch in a long innings. When you are older you have craft and judgment to pace your overall effort, as a mile runner does. He must conserve his energies for the right moment, and although I still try to crack the ball as hard as ever I have done, I spread my effort out in a much less wearing way. I played a lot better for South Australia with these new ideas than I had ever done before.

While on the subject of South Australia I must mention the great umpire who has come from that state, Colin Egar, yet another to whom spectacles have been no handicap. Egar played district cricket himself but never aspired to Sheffield Shield level. He was, however, also a very fine Australian Rules referee and he decided to concentrate on refereeing and umpiring at an early age. He quickly reached the top in umpiring and in my time at least I have never known an official who has controlled Test matches with such a consistently high level of efficiency and courtesy.

I believe one of the reasons why Egar has been so successful is that he is fit and still comparatively young. Especially in the hot-weather countries, umpiring a Test match in these days of mass publicity is as exacting as playing. Umpires have to be physically as well as mentally fit. I feel, perhaps, that in spite of the experience they acquire in the middle, first as players and then in umpiring, some English umpires are a little too old for the job six days a week. Generally, of course, the umpiring in England

Ken Barrington falls to me in the Edgbaston Test, 1963

is very good, but I do feel a move should be made to encourage more younger men to take up the job.

* * *

Sir Frank Worrell must take pride of place for the part that West Indian cricket has played in the international scene over the past few years. He has been a wonderful friend and inspiration to us all; a credit to cricketers; to cricket; and to his race.

The tours he captained to Australia in 1960 and England in 1963 did a tremendous amount to restore the game to the good graces of Australians and English folk.

I only hope I can benefit from the rich legacy he has handed on to me as the new West Indies' captain.

Frank is a gentleman by nature. Some people have charm, but it is superficial, and you can see right through it. With Worrell, the charm goes right to the bone. Because we could see how much he was respected unconditionally everywhere we knew that in him we had a leader we could look up to. I think it was our respect for Worrell which unified us as a force far more than anything else. We have had our inter-Island and Colonial jealousies and we have had our indifferent captains. But everyone agreed that playing for Frank was really something. He was always one of the boys and yet had a gift of a sort of detached greatness.

We West Indians, I suppose, are by nature a noisy, exuberant lot. We may not have long hair, but we like pop music as well as the Beatles. We sing and shout and joke, and sometimes our dressing room is a babel of noise. Yet when Frank Worrell walks into the dressing room and says, ' Just a minute

Sonny Ramadhin

107

Fiery Freddie Trueman in full action

boys ', you can hear a pin drop. He immediately has the attention of everyone.

Yes, he will be a hard man to follow, almost impossibly so. But cricketers everywhere should try to walk the Worrell way whatever their country, and the game will be all the better fo it.

The other true ' great ' with whom I have been lucky enough to rub shoulders has been Sir Donald Bradman. I only knew the Jamaican George Headley late in his career, but he must have been a marvel to have been put into the Bradman bracket by so many people. He did not have the help of other great batsmen, as the W's were able to help each other, yet he averaged around sixty often in a losing Test side and made two separate centuries in comparatively low totals in a Test at Lord's.

Headley was one of those who did not suffer by being compared with Sir Donald. Others have not been so fortunate, among them Jack Badcock, Ian Craig and Norman O'Neill. All have had thrust upon them that crushing mantle, ' The New Bradman ', and have suffered by this very unfair comparison.

I would like to think that Norman O'Neill will put the experience of the years to the best possible effect one of these days, for he has never quite lived up to his early promise. There is no more exciting batsman when the mood and form are upon him, and his fielding is superb. Perhaps he was ' over-written ' at an early age; perhaps he tries too hard.

*   *   *

Comparison with Bradman is one of the worst fates that can befall any cricketer. He was on a pinnacle in the game that had never been sighted since, perhaps, Dr. W. G. Grace was bringing cricket to the fore as a national game. He started, they say, hitting a golf ball with an old gumtree root off an old uneven wall—a natural beginning if ever there was one.

They say he failed in only one Test series of a career spanning twenty years, and that was against the so-called ' body-line ' side. I notice from *Wisden* that he failed to the extent of having an average of fifty-six for that blistering series!

Tremendous natural talent backed up by overwhelming concentration made him the heaviest scorer of all time, and I suppose he could have had Sydney Bridge just for the asking at any time in his career. I never had the luck to see him play, of course, but he did very sportingly turn out at Canberra against the M.C.C. side in 1963. It was ironic then, that even as everyone there—bowlers very much included—wanted to see him make some runs, Old Lady Cricket gave the idea an inscrutable smile, decreeing that he should be unlucky enough to score a handful, then edge one on to both pads and finally on to the wicket.

The best thing about Sir Donald, to my mind, is the interest he has shown over the years in young players. I have known him for four years and among my many regrets at leaving South Australia will be missing the kindly advice and friendship he has always shown me. Never once have I ever heard him say, ' In my day we would have done this and done that.' He merely tried to pass on his enthusiasm and knowledge without making unreasonable comparisons.

It is so easy to get discouraged by comparisons—and I certainly hope I shall never fall into the trap of thinking the game was better in my day than it will be in twenty years time.

Colin Cowdrey